TRUE CRIME
NORTHERN VIRGINIA
IN THE '50s & '60s

ZACHARY G. FORD

THE
History
PRESS

Published by The History Press
Charleston, SC
www.historypress.com

First published 2024

Manufactured in the United States

ISBN 9781467156660

Library of Congress Control Number: 2023950475

Notice: The information in this book is true and complete to the best of our knowledge. It is offered without guarantee on the part of the author or The History Press. The author and The History Press disclaim all liability in connection with the use of this book.

CONTENTS

INTRODUCTION

The suburban sprawl of Northern Virginia has seen its fair share of murderous tragedies, but rather surprisingly, there has been fairly little coverage of historic crimes that occurred in the region. As the Washington, D.C. suburbs developed in the 1950s and '60s, the character of Northern Virginia changed rather quickly into the suburban sprawl we see today. Despite the comfortable upper-middle-class security of the suburbs, with the rapid increase in population, inevitably the number of murders also increased. Some of these killings exploded across the newspapers of the times, leaving enough information to reconstruct the more dramatic of these crimes in some detail. While they seized the public imagination in their day, most of these historic murders have faded from the region's collective memory. This book aims in a small and respectful way to rediscover some of the true crimes that the Northern Virginia suburbs saw in their early decades. In selecting the particular stories in this book, I have attempted to capture a variety of events that perhaps say something about the broad range of the human condition as it relates to murder or may say something about the times in which they occurred. Some are simply unusual or intriguing.

"YOU'VE GOT IT COMING"

Unrequited love has been the cause of many a man's problems, but "kill-crazy" cab driver Walter S. Clark resolved his unreturned affections in an irrational and deadly 1954 rampage. The thirty-four-year-old Clark, an Alexandria resident described as a quiet bachelor, was infatuated with Lorraine E. Schultz, age twenty-five. The problem was, there was also a Mr. Schultz, thirty-one-year-old Herman J. Schultz. Married almost seven years, they resided off Old Telegraph Road near Groveton in Fairfax County, close to the U.S. Coast Guard Station, with four-year-old son Herman Jr. and two-year-old daughter Teresa. The family was having a run of bad luck, with Herman having lost his truck driver job shortly before Christmas. Clark met Mrs. Schultz three years earlier when he frequented an Alexandria restaurant next to his employer, Diamond Cab; Lorraine worked there as a waitress. According to one later account, Clark's attention may not have been entirely unwelcome, as apparently "she told her husband she had gone out with him several times.…She insisted, however, that she didn't want to see him" any further. Whatever tensions existed were evidently straightened out, as Clark became a family friend and was invited by the Schultz family to their house on occasion to have coffee and watch TV.

However, Clark eventually developed an ever-growing interest in Lorraine that she evidently did not reciprocate. As Mr. Schultz put it, Clark "wanted to be familiar with my wife" and the friendship ended. Seeing that his affection was not appreciated, Clark began a campaign of harassment against the Schultzes. He broke house windows, tore down their clothesline, "dragging the clothes in the dirt," slit the tires and cut the brake lines on Mr. Schultz's truck, got into fisticuffs with Schultz, followed Lorraine and her father into a market in Washington, D.C.—the litany of bad behavior went on and only worsened. At one point, he ambushed the Schultzes in their car, taking potshots at them, and on another occasion forced Lorraine's car off the road, grabbed two-year-old Teresa and drove off with her, leading Lorraine to follow him and retrieve her baby. Incredibly, the Schultzes insisted that they had tried to get warrants taken out on Clark many times, only to be "turned down." Amid their attempts to get a warrant drawn up, Clark gave them a chilling warning: if they took out a warrant, "I'll kill every damn one of you."

Finally, a warrant was issued for felonious assault after Clark showed up at the Schultz house and "blazed away with a shotgun" while Mr. and Mrs. Schultz had to crawl through an adjacent field to avoid the gunfire. Appearing before Justice Robert Fitzgerald, Clark amazingly managed to escape with a twelve-month suspended sentence and one-hundred-dollar fine; even this slap on the wrist was enough to instigate Clark's hatred toward Fitzgerald, as later events would prove. Evidently, Fitzgerald was inclined to have Clark face a grand jury, but he was convinced by Clark's lawyer to accept a misdemeanor guilty plea. Fitzgerald later referred to Clark as "ornery, mean and with as cold an eye as I've ever seen." Apparently, Clark tried to insist that Lorraine reciprocated his affection, as a newspaper account noted that at the hearing she firmly denied that she loved him. Oddly, another newspaper article reported that Lorraine "didn't want to prosecute," which doesn't make much sense given their attempts to get a warrant.

Clark's behavior, not surprisingly, did not change. On Friday, January 8, the Schultzes made another attempt to get a warrant after Clark smashed one of their house windows with a rock. Mr. and Mrs. Schultz went to the Groveton police station but were told that the police didn't issue warrants and were directed to the local justice of the peace, Harry Shepeard. Justice Shepeard declined their request, later justifying his actions by saying that there had been "so much getting of warrants" by the Schultzes. Clearly, he did not see it as a serious matter and referred them back to Robert Fitzgerald, who could revoke Clark's suspended sentence. Mr. Schultz later recalled telling Shepeard that when "somebody gets killed, then maybe you'll make up your minds to do something about this."

Around 1:30 p.m. on Saturday, January 9, Mr. Schultz and Lorraine's brother William N. Brown Jr. drove toward Arrington's Grocery after lunch, a mile away from the Schultz home. Four-year-old Herman Jr. rode in the back seat. Evidently, car trouble occurred near the intersection of Old Telegraph and Hayfield Roads, only about a quarter mile from the Schultz house, and the two men began to work on the car. Soon, a taxi, driven by none other than Walter Clark, approached the intersection. Clark was ready to follow through with his murderous threat, having borrowed a 16-gauge pump-action shotgun from a fellow cab driver "to go hunting" and purchased a box of twenty-five shells for the shotgun. Clark's mother later said he spent Friday night with her, but it would seem that he must have found out about the possibility of getting his suspended sentence revoked. Or perhaps there was no rational explanation for the final explosion of his disturbed anger that happened to erupt on this day.

With no preamble, Clark stopped, exited his taxi with the shotgun and opened fire from a distance of twenty yards. Schultz stated that the first shot "took my hat right off," blasting apart the brim, and he promptly took off running. Brother-in-law Brown gamely threw a rock at Clark's head but missed. Undeterred, Clark followed Schultz, hitting him with a blast in his

Herman Schultz, his son and his brother-in-law pulled over at this spot. Walter Clark drove up from the left and opened fire as they fled through what are now school athletic fields. *Author's collection.*

right shoulder and another in his left hand. Brown kept up his rock barrage until Clark turned on him; he sprinted away and thought he lost Clark in the overgrown field until he suddenly came face to face with him, giving Clark the chance to fire into Brown's foot. Clark returned to his cab with his plan of revenge only beginning. After Clark drove off, Schultz returned to his car and picked up his undoubtedly frightened son. He then proceeded to the house of a neighbor and called the police. Leaving Herman Jr. with the neighbor, he sprinted toward his house, but police were already arriving at the scene when he ran up. It was too late.

In Schultz's absence, Clark pulled up to the house in his taxi; entering the living room, Clark shot Lorraine in the face. She was holding two-year-old Teresa, who tumbled to the floor and sustained a "deep forehead cut." Lorraine's mother, Edna B. Brown, had the misfortune of visiting the home that day, and Clark shot her in the throat as she tried to flee the kitchen onto the back porch. She collapsed in the doorway and died on the spot. His thirst for revenge satisfied for the moment, Clark fled in his taxi. The winded Mr. Schultz ran into the house, past the arriving police and immediately saw his wife lying on the floor; he collapsed beside her.

Clark drove to the Dewey Park subdivision road a mile away, followed it a quarter mile to its end and abandoned his car. In the much more rural Fairfax County of 1954, he fled through the woods to an old ten-by-ten-foot "chicken shed" near the northern perimeter of Fort Belvoir, atop a hill about half a mile from the Schultz house. A sawmill owned by Mrs. H.A. Melton stood nearby. Fairfax County, Alexandria and Virginia State police forces descended on the area in search of Clark, reinforced by an ever-growing posse of armed locals intent on finding the killer. Newspapers later estimated that 150 to 200 armed men, uniformed and civilian, were searching a nine-square-mile area, aided by bloodhounds and equipped with "long-range weapons." About two hours after the shootings, Clark's abandoned cab was found; inside was a note to Justice Robert Fitzgerald, who had the given the fine and suspended sentence in Clark's assault case: "Notice to Judge Fitzgerald. You are the cause of this. You'll get it, too. You've got it coming." The police immediately dispatched a guard to Fitzgerald's house.

Part of the posse came upon Clark's chicken shed lair, and Officer Dennis R. O'Neil looked into the shack to check it out while five other officers covered him. Peering inside with his service pistol drawn, the startled officer saw Clark crouched down and looking back at him. Clark and O'Neil exchanged a furious blaze of gunfire at a distance of six feet; O'Neil was hit in the shoulder but got off three shots before staggering away from the shed. The other five police officers, joined by eager members of the civilian posse, opened fire, unleashing "at least 150 shots…from rifles, shotguns, pistols, and a submachine gun." An officer eventually got the fusillade to cease, and the posse cautiously approached the shack. Clark's shot-up body was dragged outside, riddled with fifteen to twenty bullet wounds. Seventeen unfired shells remained in his pockets, loaded with No. 6 and No. 8 shot. The quick-shooting Officer O'Neil eventually recovered after spending several days recuperating in the hospital.

Police searched Clark's body and found a bloodstained note, written on the back of an envelope:

> *I hope God will forgive me, some day, but I loved her so much, and she loved me but everybody was in the way. Notice[:] please some good FBI agents investigate Judge Fitzgerald in Fairfax. He caused this tragedy too. Mr. Moore[,] William Brown hit your cab[,] fix him. Darling, I'll be with you some place.*

Left: Killer Walter Clark lies among more respectable veterans at Arlington National Cemetery. The author suspects he is one of very few people to ever visit his grave. *Author's collection.*

Right: Lorraine Schultz lies only a few hundred yards away from Clark's grave, the two bizarrely united in death. *Author's collection.*

As if his obsession with Fitzgerald was not bizarre enough, the fact that he bothered in his last moments to blame Schultz's in-law William Brown for supposedly denting his cab certainly says something about his disordered state of mind.

While Herman Schultz and William Brown were being treated in the hospital, Clark's brother Julian visited Schultz in hospital to extend his condolences. Julian said the family bore the police "no ill-will for shooting his brother." The now motherless Schultz children went to stay with a sister of Lorraine; Herman Schultz apparently had been released from the hospital and was staying with friends but evidently did not feel up to the task of watching his children. Unfortunately, Lorraine's sister "became upset" and deposited Teresa and Herman Jr.—along with her own seven children—with a friend, who had three children of her own. Fortunately, the kindly friend was willing to look after twelve children, saying, "Well, somebody's got to do it, and I've got a big house. We all had roast beef for dinner, and it was good, too." While this family drama played out, a morbid scene occurred at the Schultz house, with "steady stream of curiosity seekers" braving a rainstorm to peer through the windows at the bloodstained floors.

A joint funeral service was held for Lorraine and her mother, with Mrs. Brown interred in Bethel Cemetery, Alexandria, and Lorraine in Arlington National Cemetery; Herman Schultz had served as a corporal in the U.S. Marine Corps. While Lorraine's grave notes that she was the wife of "H.J. Schultz," he apparently is not buried at Arlington. There was another interment scheduled at Arlington: Walter Clark's. He had served honorably as a sergeant in the Army Air Forces during World War II, entitling him to his grave in Arlington. He lies there today, within sight of President Kennedy's grave—and only a few hundred yards from Lorraine's resting place.

2

"SHARE YE ONE ANOTHER'S BURDENS"

On one Saturday morning in April 1959, the peace of a quiet subdivision in Springfield was shattered by an unthinkable tragedy in which a seemingly contented family man attacked his family in a murderous rage. Forty-one-year-old Joseph B. Matthews Jr., described as a "model citizen, an ideal husband and father, a particularly happy suburbanite," lived at 6505 Highland Avenue with his wife, Helen, and their three children: thirteen-year-old Susan and twelve-year-old twins Sharon and Steven. An engineer with the Federal Aviation Administration (FAA), Joe seemed to have a happy and comfortable life in the suburbs. Neighbors and friends remembered an idyllic family life. Joe was a Little League umpire and enjoyed singing while his wife and children accompanied him on instruments. He could often be seen playing sports with his children in the backyard and enjoyed cooking out, frequently inviting friends over. The children were known to be "polite and well-behaved," and one neighbor commented, "My husband and I always hoped our children would be as model teen-agers as they were." Sharon was popular and had been president of the sixth grade class in the previous year and currently was captain of the school's safety patrol. The family was active at Grace Presbyterian Church, where Joe was a deacon and director of the youth choir. Reverend Robert J. McMullen Jr. said all community service projects were given to Matthews to run "and he handled them ably." His role as head of the church's committee to help the needy and those in trouble would prove sadly ironic. He was also a member of a church singing quartet called Grace Notes, and outside of church he sang with a barbershop group called the Fairfax Jubilairs.

Joe certainly seemed to be a success story. After graduating from high school in New York City and from Lehigh University with a bachelor of science degree in physics, he married Helen in July 1940. In 1941, the young couple moved to D.C., where he worked for the Navy's Bureau of Aeronautics in research and development. When war broke out, he went into the navy as a lieutenant and spent most of the war on engineering projects in Washington. He was in Honolulu, en route to an assignment with an air group on Okinawa, when the war ended, and he then returned to his civilian job with the navy. Eventually, he moved on to a job with the Airways Modernization Board, which then became part of the FAA, where he worked at the Development Division of the Bureau of Research and Development, located at 7th and D Streets SW in Washington. It was noted that while "Mr. Matthews had a warm personality and many friends he did not talk much about his work." Interestingly, one article described his FAA work as "'sensitive' from a national security standpoint," but it's unclear to what extent this was actually true. Evidently, he worked on developing navigational devices for civil airlines.

Friday, April 10, would later be reconstructed in as much detail as possible. Matthews took the day off from work, saying he felt tired—an act ominous in hindsight but not something that alarmed Helen at the time. On that Friday, he worked in the yard with his wife and appeared "carefree." He also repaired a bike for Helen, worked with Steven on his train set and played ping-pong with daughter Susan, giving no cause for concern. That night, he played chess with the family in their home and said something to his wife about "going back to New Jersey and finding a job" according to his mother; presumably, Helen later relayed this strange statement to her. That night, he got up from bed several times, but when Helen asked him about it Saturday morning, he said he had gotten plenty of sleep. Sharon worked as a babysitter that night for a neighbor and was looking forward to attending a baseball game on Saturday.

That same day, Helen quit her job as secretary of Lorton Elementary in order to spend more time at home, driven by a recent incident involving their daughter Susan. Susan had been suspended for two weeks with several other students at Lee High School for taking a bottle of her father's vodka and bringing it to school, although Reverend McMullen said it was simply a prank and Susan was a "fine, intelligent girl." Her principal agreed that she was a good student and not a troublemaker. However, the incident had been "profoundly upsetting" for Joe Matthews and in hindsight seems to have been a major trigger for what was to happen. Joe was so disturbed that he tried to resign as a deacon at Grace Presbyterian but was talked out of it. Joe also mentioned the incident to his boss, who told him not to worry about it.

Saturday morning, April 11, was "so peaceful" according to Helen, with Joe coming downstairs and talking with her at about 7:30. Joe sat at the table talking with her about the morning's rain effect on the plants in their yard as she made orange juice. Son Steven said he wanted to go bowling, and Joe gave him $1.50 and talked to his daughter about the baseball game she was attending later that day. He said he wanted only coffee for breakfast and left the room. Helen later thought he was gone for five to ten minutes. The children entered their "small dining room," the girls in bathrobes with their backs to the living room and Steven in "sports shirt and slacks" with his back to the kitchen. Orange juice, cereal, milk and eggs were spread on the table when she called for her husband to come back to get his coffee. She had her back to the living room as she turned to sit down across from Steven. The next events would be reconstructed as best they could, seemingly too full of action to have really played out in the few explosive moments that they did.

Joe suddenly came in from the living room, wildly swinging Steven's

The Matthews house stands little-changed today. The Whiteheads lived in the house to the right and the Lees to the left. *Author's collection.*

baseball bat, normally found in the family's playroom. He knocked Susan from her chair first; Helen screamed and tried to stop him and was struck across the face, causing what were later described as "severe facial lacerations, a fractured nose, and shock." It all happened so fast that the children did not have time to flee as he continually rained blows on them. Helen later recalled that Joe was "swinging the bat so fast I could hardly see it."

"Bleeding profusely," she ran to their next-door neighbor at 6507 Highland, who fortunately was an FBI agent named Richard C. Whitehead; he recalled the time as about 8:15 a.m. Whitehead's wife recalled that Helen pounded on the door and shouted, "Help me! Help me! Joe has gone mad. He's beating the children." Mrs. Whitehead used a towel to staunch Helen's bleeding as Mr. Whitehead ran to the home of John Lee on the other side of the Matthews house to enlist help. Lee was "just getting up," so Whitehead yelled at Lee's wife to "send him next door" as Whitehead ran to the Matthews house and entered by the side door. He later said that as he "approached all I heard were thuds. I opened the door. It was awful.…Joe was standing over the girls, the bat still in his hand." In a moment that must have stayed with him for the rest of his life, Whitehead made eye contact with Matthews, who said, "Dick, I'm sorry. Kill me. Shoot me, Dick." Whitehead replied, "Joe, give me the bat," and Matthews gave it to him without resistance. Suddenly, Matthews dashed into the kitchen, turned his back and cut his throat with a kitchen knife. He turned and calmly walked back into the dining room to lie down next to Sharon. In a surreal moment, he began reciting the Lord's Prayer "but never finished it."

At this point, Mrs. Lee ran in and called the police from the Matthews's phone, soon followed by Mr. Lee. At 8:22 a.m., Fairfax County police officer Herbert C. Anderson received a call on his car radio about a "fight" at the Matthews's address; he was about a mile and a half away and saw Mr. Whitehead "waving frantically" to him from the front yard as he pulled up. Anderson ran in and saw Steven "lying in the corner by the kitchen door" with the girls on the floor beside the table; Joe was still lying next to Sharon. The officer then left the house to talk to Whitehead and check on Helen. Franconia volunteer rescue squad member Bill Clardy arrived a few minutes later in his own car; he had heard the ambulance dispatch call from his nearby house, so he responded.

He glanced inside and went to get his medical equipment; as he began working on Sharon, he got a shock as suddenly "Matthews got up and began waving his arms.…I realized I was alone in the house with him and didn't know what he might do.…I let out a yell and the officer came into the house again, hit him on the head with a nightstick and knocked him down. Later he had to handcuff him." Whitehead recalled Joe at this point looking "half-crazy, sort of mad.…He seemed belligerent when he got up." After Officer Anderson subdued Joe, Whitehead told Clardy about Mrs. Matthews next door and he went to see her. Helen was being comforted by Mrs. Whitehead and kept muttering that she needed to get back to her house and "Poor Joe." She had "a gash over one eye and a big swelling.…She asked about her family and I had to lie to her." Clardy told her the girls were "all right" and only the boy was "pretty bad." To Clardy, it "seemed like hours before more help came…but it was only a minute or two before Bill Rothrock arrived in his car to help me." Rothrock was another volunteer rescue squad member who also responded to the scene. Two Annandale and Franconia ambulances soon arrived, but Steven was already dead and Joe died on the

Youthful hijinks from Susan Matthews precipitated her father's explosion of violence. Here she poses with her school's Latin club shortly before her death. She is seated on the left in the second row from the front. *From the 1959 Lee High School Yearbook.*

way to hospital. The girls died less than an hour later in the emergency room at about 9:45 a.m. Police Chief William Durrer arrived, and just as he started talking to reporters in front of the house, word arrived of the deaths at the hospital; the entire incident had happened "barely an hour earlier." No details about the children's injuries were ever released, other than to note that they were "so badly beaten it was impossible to tell how many times they had been struck." Thinking back to Susan's suspension and its deep effect on Joe, police thought "it was significant" that Susan was struck first.

One curious aspect of the crime scene would never be adequately explained. Two chairs were missing from the dining room, and police found them lying on their side "as a form of barrier" outside of Steven's closed room. Inside, Tinker Bell, the "part-cocker" family dog, sat on the bed, but given that the door was closed, there didn't seem to be any need for a barricade. In the few moments before neighbor Whitehead burst in, Matthews had apparently carried the "blood-spattered chairs across the living room and up six steps to the bedroom." While one can presume he intentionally put the family dog in the closed room before the murders to prevent any interference with the killings, his reason for deliberately carrying the chairs up there in the moments after the attack probably defies any rational explanation.

Reverend McMullen broke the news of her children's deaths to Mrs. Matthews at the hospital, but due to her condition she showed "little emotion." In the hospital, Mrs. Matthews agonized over her split-second decision that deadly morning and kept saying, "If only I hadn't left the house for help, I might have been able to protect my children." In reality, she almost certainly would have just wound up as another fatality. Joe's father was contacted by phone in New York. Grace, Joe's mother, described her ex-husband as being "terribly upset," and he began to make travel plans even though he was suffering from Parkinson's disease. Grasping for answers, Helen requested an autopsy be conducted on her husband. Alexandria coroner John A. Sims agreed to the autopsy since it "may give her peace of mind and satisfy her," but it was clear that doctors did not expect to find any medical explanations for Joe's actions. Helen hoped "that a brain tumor or some other physical reason would be found for his violent act." A tumor at least could offer some explanation for the terrible tragedy. After the April 12 autopsy, Dr. Richard Palmer, chief pathologist at Alexandria Hospital, said that he "found nothing of any significance that would explain Mr. Matthew's actions" and that while a "detailed microscopic study of the brain tissue" would be conducted in a few days, he did not expect to find anything of note. Helen was still in the hospital under sedation while, rather ghoulishly, "reporters waited in the hospital corridor," but "the distraught widow declined requested interviews."

As Helen continued to recover at the hospital, Police Chief Durrer closed the case but noted that they "know no more about the real reason why it happened than we did early Saturday morning....I don't think anybody knows." Cremation for all four dead family members was scheduled for the thirteenth with a funeral service at Grace Presbyterian followed by burial at Arlington National Cemetery. More than 240 people attended the service at Grace Presbyterian on the fifteenth, including Helen. At the service, Reverend McMullen delivered a

The bloody baseball bat used by Joseph Matthews to kill his children and the knife he used to cut his own throat are carried out of the house by a detective. *From the* Northern Virginia Sun.

message simply titled "Why?" and he said, "This tragedy has reminded us of the weakness in us....We come here with a sense of guilt, wondering wherein we have failed." Apparently, Joe's father did attend the funeral along with Grace and several other relatives. McMullen asked Helen if she had anything to add to his sermon, and she simply said, "Enjoy your kids." At the conclusion of his message, McMullen urged the attendees to "share ye one another's burdens."

After the unexpected events of April 11, friends and investigators tried to understand Joe's mindset in the weeks leading up to the tragedy. Small incidents that were overlooked at the time suddenly held looming portent, strung together with other hints of impending trouble that made sense only in hindsight. Investigators and psychiatrists pondered and debated over Joe's mental state, but most agreed that his "major problem was that he kept things too much to himself" and he lacked a "safety valve" for his emotions. A psychiatrist who had been a "personal friend of his for years" said there was "not a clue, not a hint" of something wrong and added, "If a thing like this can happen to Joe Matthews, it can happen to anyone." One neighbor recalled that "Matthews kept everything real deep inside." After the fact, psychiatrists saw signs of depression; it wasn't the life problems themselves that were too great for him to deal with, it was his inability to deal with them in a healthy way and ask for help. Some speculated that his actions were driven more by suicidal than murderous impulses, and others thought a fugue state might be to blame. Helen confirmed that he had complained of feeling tired lately and that he was "letting the children get on his nerves." In hindsight, there did seem to be signs of depression. As Helen told Joe's mother, Grace, "Joe had been upset periodically in the past couple of years but she said he always pulled out of his depressed moods and never showed a tendency to violence." No doubt indicative of the culture that must have contributed to Joe's reticence is the fact that the phrase *mental illness* shows up in a single newspaper piece: a letter to the editor.

As one newspaper writer noted, in "the last days of his life, particularly the final week, there were indications of the coming storm, but at the time they seemed nothing serious." Earlier that week, Joe commented to his fellow Grace Notes members at their weekly practice that he was "not feeling well" and his eyes were bothering him, but the group saw no cause for concern. One of the group members described him as a "casual relaxed person…never raised his voice" and saw nothing to change that assessment in the week before the murders. He saw the family doctor about headaches and fatigue and was recommended for a "general checkup," which he planned to do. His boss, Alexander Winick, chief of the Research and Development Bureau of the Navigation Division, FAA, said Joe had been "somewhat withdrawn recently" at work. Winick asked him if something was wrong, and he said his eyes were bothering him; there were no concerns over his job, and Winick said he was a "highly qualified specialist."

Helen was driven home by relatives on April 15, "silent, composed and weary" and still wearing bandages. Church members had cleaned the Matthews house and put away the children's clothes and belongings; flowers "crowded the living room." Helen was not bitter toward her husband, and McMullen said she was "trying to find a new usefulness in life." She expressed interest in working with young people and planned to go away for the weekend with her sister but intended to return to Springfield to live. It is hard to disagree with McMullen's assessment that she was "a brave and strong woman." Helen's brother was grateful for McMullen's efforts, calling him "an extraordinary man."

Fairfax County detectives interviewed Helen to see about Matthews's actions in the last few months; afterward, they talked to reporters. Detective Corporal Marvin H. Herrel said that Joe had been taking pills, "something like tranquilizers," in the preceding week for headaches and fatigue. The pills had been issued only last week to tide him over until he could get a complete physical exam. Police talked to the doctor who prescribed the pills, Dr. Joseph Atchison, and confirmed that they were a "mild sedative" that had been given to "ease tensions" but contained nothing that should have caused his actions. Apparently, Joe had taken the medication, because a "small, empty medicine vial" was found on the floor at the home. Helen did not know about the pills, but all in all, it doesn't seem as though they could have had much bearing on the tragedy. The vial measured only one and a half inches by one and a half inches, so it could hardly have held many pills. Dr. Atchison also referred to medicine he had given Joe for arthritis pain last June and that he renewed that last week. The doctor said it was similar to aspirin and also should not have had any effect on Joe's mental state. One potentially odd fact came up: Joe told the doctor that his last check-up was about six months earlier, but in fact, records showed that it had been in February 1957. Perhaps more relevant, investigators looked into his medical records and found that in 1948 he was treated for "chronic nervous exhaustion and fatigue," which was while he was attending night school for a master's degree at George Washington University and simultaneously working a day job, but nothing else suspicious. It's hard to know exactly what the diagnosis entailed, but it is hard not to see it as a warning sign of mental troubles.

Matthews had been negotiating a $125,000 contract in the last few weeks for developing an air navigation computer, which could well have been a contributor to his stress, but his work had remained excellent. Investigators checked to see if financial problems may have added to his troubles but found nothing out of order. He was a GS-14 making $11,355 to $13,275 a year depending on years of service. In today's purchasing power, this translates to roughly $114,000 to $133,000, so he was quite comfortable and apparently always lived carefully within a budget.

An intriguing hint at a possible contributing factor to the tragedy surfaced: Joe "gave up drinking entirely" as a result of Susan's suspension. Police were told (presumably by Helen or family friends) that "he had been accustomed to drinking at home in the evening and the sudden cut-off was worse for him than a gradual tapering off. In a sense…he was suffering from 'withdrawal' symptoms." One report took it further, saying that Matthews had mentioned the fear of becoming an alcoholic to friends "casually from time to time" due to his "tendency to drink frequently by himself in his home, often after his family had gone to bed." Police "heard" (but didn't give a source) that he "had been drinking heavily several months ago but they no longer considered it a problem because he exercised the willpower to quit." Somewhat contradictorily, Police Chief Durrer also said that Matthews had been a "social drinker." Taken together, it certainly seems that there was more to Joe's drinking than just social drinking; certainly, self-medicating with alcohol would not

Joseph Matthews lies in Arlington Cemetery in the same grave as the children he killed. *Author's collection.*

be uncommon for someone suffering from anxiety or depression and could not have improved his situation.

Inevitably, one is inclined to examine Joe's early years for indications that the seeds of the tragedy were planted in his childhood. The only potentially suggestive element for the amateur psychiatrist is perhaps his inferred relationship, or lack thereof, with his father. Joe was born in Batavia, Dutch East Indies (now Jakarta, Indonesia), on November 8, 1917, to missionary parents. He was three when he returned to the United States, and his parents divorced when he was young. After interviewing Joe's mother, Grace, a local paper reported that he and his three siblings lived "in various parts of the country, mostly in Tennessee and New Jersey." One can infer that Joe's father, Joseph B. Matthews Sr., was not a large part of his life, as he married twice more following his divorce from Grace. Since Joe was apparently raised primarily by his mother, it is not surprising that at the time of the murders she lived a handful of miles away in Arlington while Joe's father lived in New York City. Moreover, as Joe grew into adulthood, the elder Matthews was on an unusual career trajectory that kept him busy.

While a detailed biography of Joseph B. Matthews Sr. is far outside the scope of this story, a brief overview of his rather unconventional life is perhaps suggestive of his relative absence from his son's life. The one-time

Methodist minister became increasingly involved in far left-wing causes, traveled to the Soviet Union multiple times and in fact popularized the term *fellow traveler* when he wrote his memoir about his break with Communism. In the late 1930s, he pivoted drastically to anti-Communism and became the research director for the House Special Committee on Un-American Activities, emerging as one of the country's leading anti-Communist investigators. In 1953, he was appointed as the research director for Senator Joseph McCarthy's Senate Committee but had to resign after a national uproar followed the publication of an article he wrote for *Mercury* magazine in which the former minister stated the "largest single group supporting the Communist apparatus in the United States is composed of Protestant clergy." Joe's father was nationally famous for a time, and many of the news reports on the tragedy include references to him. Was Joe's habit of internalizing his feelings and seeking to be the perfect family man a reaction to his extroverted, unconventional father?

Echoes of the Matthews tragedy surfaced in February 1964 when Thomas Cox, an elementary school principal, returned to his Falls

The three children's shared date of death hints at the tragedy that befell them. One wonders if a passing visitor has ever taken notice and pondered at their fate. *Author's collection.*

Church home after work and found that his wife, Judith, had shot their four children and then turned the gun on herself. While a shocking story in Northern Virginia, it seems to not have generated quite the same bewilderment as the Matthews killings when it was revealed that Judith Cox had been diagnosed with depression severe enough that she was hospitalized for an extended period. People were evidently able to process that someone with a serious mental illness might act out in this way, while the seemingly happy and undiagnosed Joe Matthews would forever remain an enigma.

However one might speculate, Joe's mother, Grace, made as reasonable an assessment as anyone, saying, "He was a quiet type of person who liked to read a lot.…I couldn't have asked for a more wonderful son. If someone else had troubles they would go to Joe and he would help them—but he never seemed to discuss his own problems." She added, "I feel that my son was sick" but no one knew it; she hoped that it "will help someone else who is having problems. Maybe they will go for help before it is too late. One's own family sometimes doesn't know about other's problems. Sometimes people don't even know themselves."

3

THE KILLER TWO-YEAR-OLD

Lillian Chastain almost got away with murder. The Prince William County sheriff was willing to write off her husband's death as suicide, but she could not just leave well enough alone; she wanted the insurance money. Early on June 11, 1959, police received a phone call that Truett Chastain had been shot in his home off Route 621 near rural Bristow. When they arrived at the five-room frame home he had built less than a year earlier, they found the thirty-year-old man lying in bed, covered with his bedsheets. His twenty-seven-year-old wife of nine years, Lillian, explained that while making breakfast she heard a gunshot, ran to the bedroom and found their two-year-old daughter, Wilma Lee, "sitting astride his body" while holding a loaded Smith & Wesson revolver. According to Lillian, Truett gasped, "I can't breathe, Lillian, I can't breathe," and she ran out of the room to call an ambulance. By the time she returned after placing the call, Truett was dead. The revolver was apparently kept in a "shoe bag" hanging three feet from the floor in the bedroom closet. Lillian said Wilma knew there was a "favorite pair of new shoes" in the bag and a high chair was pushed against the open door. In her telling, the two-year-old had moved the high chair to the closet, climbed up, opened the bag, retrieved the gun and shot her father. Mrs. Chastain added that Wilma Lee had gotten up in the night to sleep with her parents, which she often did. But the odd tale of the murderous two-year-old didn't seem to give Sheriff Turner D. Wheeling much pause.

In fairness, Sheriff Wheeling evidently did find the death suspicious, as he not only had the body sent to Alexandria Hospital for the autopsy but also collected a pathologist's report from Dr. Geoffrey Mann, Virginia's chief medical examiner, which seems to be rather high level for a death in rural Prince William County. The fact that Truett had been shot in the left side of his chest, with his daughter supposedly sharing the bed with him, would have made for an unusual suicide, but that is what Sheriff Wheeling decided. Also weighing heavily in his decision-making was the fact that the .32-caliber revolver had a twelve-and-a-half-pound trigger pull, which could not have been pulled by the two-year-old. Powder marks were on the bedsheets, and the revolver was loaded except for the one expended round. Sheriff Wheeling also said the "course of the bullet" and the fact that Chastain had financial problems led to his suicide ruling. Once he eliminated Wilma Lee as the guilty party, it would seem obvious to logically consider whether Lillian had in fact been the one to pull the trigger, but the thought apparently did not cross the sheriff's mind. That Lillian seemed intent on blaming her young child rather than agree that his death was a suicide perhaps should have set off some alarms as well. Despite already declaring the death a suicide, Wheeling did conduct paraffin tests on the hands of Truett and Wilma Lee, with the results expected in ten days. That he evidently did not see the need to conduct a similar test on Lillian's hands says a great deal about the depth of the shambolic "investigation." The situation got even murkier in early August, when in the midst of an effort to collect on her husband's life insurance policy, Lilian refused to accept Sheriff Wheeling's findings and "objected to a suicide ruling in her husband's death in order to collect insurance." Again, one would think this would cause the sheriff to look more closely at Mrs. Chastain, but he simply backtracked and declared the case to still be open. While all of this was occurring, Mrs. Chastain moved with her supposedly murderous two-year-old and three other children to neighboring Stafford County while she tried to claim the insurance payout.

The story suddenly broke open in late February 1960. At the beginning of the year, a new sheriff, Ralph Shumate, took office and soon reopened the case due to "repeated requests from the dead man's family and the wife's family, and because he was not convinced that the original investigation had revealed the entire story." He contacted the Virginia State Police and the Fairfax County Police Department for assistance in his investigation. Sheriff Shumate was already proving himself rather sharper than his predecessor. The new investigators spoke to Lillian, and she agreed to go to Fairfax for a lie detector test. Immediately following the lie detector test, Lillian confessed to shooting her husband. The state police investigator, Jack Hall, said she "had gotten to the point where she had to tell somebody." As Lillian acknowledged, "I was tired with the whole mess and wanted to get it over with.…You can't live with something like that." In a written confession, she said she shot Truett "in a fit of anger" after an early morning argument over money. She added that if "I'd known what I was doing I would never have picked up the gun. I didn't realize I was so under pressure.…I am not sure what my mental standing was at the time. As soon as I'd done it, I realized what I'd done." At the court hearing that followed her confession, she entered her plea in a voice "barely audible above the ticking of the

Lillian Truett was tried in the historic Prince William County Courthouse in Manassas. *Author's collection.*

clock" in the Prince William County Courthouse. She told Judge Arthur Sinclair that "there's no doubt about it your Honor, no point in requiring the Commonwealth to prove it." She only had one desire: "The only thing I want, sir, is to go back to my children as soon as possible." Her four children were now living with her parents in Staunton, her hometown. There was no word on how young Wilma Lee felt about no longer having a murder rap against her.

While she seemed calm when confessing to the judge, after she was denied bond, Lillian cut her left wrist with a piece of broken mirror from a makeup compact. It apparently was not a terribly serious injury, but the wound was bandaged and any potentially dangerous items were removed from her cell, with jailers checking on her every hour. A sanity committee was held to determine her mental state, but they saw no evidence of mental illness and "refused to commit her for observation." At her sentencing hearing on April 22, Judge Sinclair rather generously gave her the minimum sentence: five years in the state penitentiary. Lillian stood quietly and "sobbed softly" as she was led away. Virginia parole laws meant that Lillian would not necessarily even serve five years, and by January 1965, she was living in Miami, Florida, and working as a department store clerk. Presumably, she was trying to restart her life in an entirely new place, but there was not to be a happy ending. Her death certificate boils down a sad tale to a few words and bears the rather ironic designation of her marital status as "widowed." On the afternoon of January 4, 1965, Lillian "ingested numerous medications, including phenobarbital [and] librium" in what the medical examiner found to be a clear case of suicide through "barbituate intoxication." Lillian evidently lingered at a local hospital until early on the morning of January 7 before passing away. Her body was returned to Virginia, where she rests in Augusta County, sharing a headstone with the man she killed, Truett Chastain.

4

LIFE IS CHEAP

VIGNETTES OF NEEDLESS DEATHS

A Game of William Tell

A three-hour drinking session led to the demise of J. Lee "Pat" Murphy, a forty-eight-year-old father of two, on December 13, 1960. Murphy; an employee, George Thomas Selecman Jr.; and a mutual friend named Robert Glass were welcoming the holiday season in the office of the junkyard owned by Murphy near the small community of Hoadley in Prince William County. At some point, "one of the most high-powered hunting rifles known" was introduced into the mix and disaster followed. While Murphy was evidently intoxicated, Glass later testified that Selecman "definitely wasn't drunk," making his actions even more head-scratching. The conversation turned to boasts about who was the best marksman, and Murphy challenged Selecman to shoot the hat off his head. Selecman initially declined the challenge, but Murphy called him a "chicken," so Selecman loaded a .300 Magnum round into the hunting rifle and put a bullet through the crown of Murphy's felt hat. Murphy took his turn next, "shooting apart a canvas hunting cap pulled down tightly on Selecman's head."

Glass, obviously the smartest of the three, stepped outside the office at this point, not wanting to see more. But the inevitable soon happened, and Murphy wound up with a bullet in his head. Knowing what the scream and shot meant, Glass looked inside the office and saw Murphy lying on the floor and Selecman saying, "Oh my God. What have I done? I've shot a man." The police were called, and obviously realizing the trouble he was in, Selecman told the responding officer that Murphy tried to grab the gun from him and it went off. Selecman was indicted at a February 6 grand jury hearing for a June 20 trial. The prosecuting attorney tried to frame Selecman's actions as an ego trip gone bad, saying he "killed Murphy because he feared the next shot would be his turn to die." Evidently, he could not bring himself to step outside and declare defeat. His defense attorney, Thomas M. Moncure of Stafford, insisted it was an accident.

Initially charged with murder, at his June trial Selecman agreed to plead guilty to involuntary manslaughter and was given a year's suspended penitentiary sentence. Murphy was described as a "lifelong friend" to him, and Murphy's wife, father and sister asked that no further action be taken. In the fifteen-minute trial, Judge Calvin VanDyke said the yearlong penitentiary sentence would not be invoked as long as "good behavior" continued. Apparently, Selecman did stay out of trouble and presumably selected less risky games of chance in the future.

For a Bottle of Wine

A woodland drinking party had deadly results for Thomas Scott on June 2, 1961. That summer evening, several men were passing around some liquor in the woods near Gallows Road in Fairfax County when a dispute erupted over the ownership of a bottle of wine. Frank "Buck" Jackson, a fifty-six-year-old Merrifield man, pulled a .32-caliber pistol and put a round into the neck of forty-one-year-old Thomas Scott, "an acquaintance." One of the other men drinking, Henry Edward Lee, said Jackson raised his hand, a loud noise followed and Scott fell. Jackson claimed Scott hit him, he punched back with a pistol in hand, and then it was the old story of the pistol "accidentally" going off. As the other drinkers carried Scott off, Jackson tossed the pistol away and departed the scene. When later asked why he brought a gun to the drinking rendezvous, he said he was afraid of "some bad dogs" in the area and had conveniently found the pistol in his house some time before.

Then followed a tragicomedy of errors. Scott was brought to Fairfax Hospital, and Dr. John Wescott, "a resident in surgery" in charge of the emergency room, denied him entrance, presumably detecting that he was under the influence of alcohol. Scott's companions made another attempt that same night, and he was turned away again. Eighteen hours later, he was finally admitted after police officers took Scott to the hospital, where "they had to threaten to arrest the injured man before the hospital would admit him. The hospital is required to admit police prisoners." It was too late; he was "partially paralyzed" by then and died two hours later. A hospital spokesman made the rather disconcerting statement that Scott "probably would have died anyway" and that it "boils down to a difference of medical opinion." Wescott evidently told his superiors that he "thought the wound not serious" and that it "could just as well be treated the next day." To the layman, Dr. Wescott's diagnosis that a gunshot wound to the neck did not rise to the level of an emergency room visit must remain a puzzle. Police Chief William L. Durrer "lodged a protest" with the hospital, but the brouhaha seems to have quickly settled down. It turns out Wescott was simultaneously serving as resident at Fairfax, Georgetown and Arlington Hospitals and since the shooting had "left the area."

The initial hearing centered more on the circumstances of Scott's death than the perpetrator. The autopsy report was not admitted into evidence,

Frank "Buck" Jackson and several other murderers in this book faced justice at the historic Fairfax County Courthouse. *Author's collection.*

with defense lawyers and prosecutor Quin Elson simply saying he "is dead" and "had been shot." The point of the vague language was to avoid arguments over whether Scott would have survived if he had been admitted into Fairfax Hospital. The defense said the trial jury would be told of the specific events if the case went to trial. Clearly the defense strategy was to argue that Jackson had not inflicted a necessarily deadly wound and it was only the hospital's refusal to treat the wound that led to Scott's demise. At the January 1962 trial, Jackson decided to plead guilty to second-degree murder in front of Judge Paul E. Brown in Fairfax Circuit Court. His defense attorney originally asked Judge Brown to reduce the charges to manslaughter, but after hearing from witnesses, Brown declined the request. The press then seemed to lose interest in the story, not bothering to report the results of Jackson's sentencing hearing.

THE BEER THIEF

Disputed alcohol ownership likewise led to the death of twenty-five-year-old Walter Gormer Hill on November 10, 1961. At a gathering at the Herndon residence of Harry Herns at 651 Monroe Street, an argument erupted over the "ownership of several cans of beer." Thirty-nine-year-old Robert Thaxton evidently held claim to the beers, but Hill decided to take them with him as he left the party. This grossly offended Thaxton, who said Hill "had not contributed to the purchase of the beverage and had no right to take it away with him." Thaxton pulled a .32-caliber pistol and retained possession of the beer by putting a bullet into Hill's chest. The Herndon rescue responded to the scene, but Hill died at the hospital the next morning. Thaxton was held in the Fairfax jail in lieu of $15,000 bond while Hill's funeral arrangements were made at Oak Grove Baptist Church.

In a January hearing, Thaxton pleaded not guilty in front of Judge Paul E. Brown (who must have been quite exasperated after Frank Jackson's similar trial only a few days earlier). At his May trial, Thaxton not surprisingly claimed self-defense and said Hill was advancing toward him when he opened fire. The strategy did not particularly work, as he was convicted of second-degree murder and sentenced to eighteen years in prison after the jury deliberated for eleven hours.

"YOU'RE NOT GOING TO SHOOT ME, JIMMY!"

Another vice, cigarettes, led to the demise of nineteen-year-old Charles Lee in February 1964. On the twenty-ninth of that leap year, Lee was in the home of Betty Lee Carroll at 1507 Arlington Terrace in Alexandria with eighteen-year-old James Kerr and several other young men. Newspaper accounts alternately reported that Carroll, a thirty-eight-year-old widow, intended to marry either Kerr or Lee. Regardless of who was the suitor in the rather odd May-September romance, both were gathered for drinks with a number of other young men around 2:00 a.m. Lee asked Kerr for some cigarettes and was told there was a pack in Kerr's shirt pocket, hanging on a chair. The ungrateful Lee "took all but one or two which he threw on the bed towards Kerr." The indignant Kerr objected, but "Lee came over and beat Jimmy in the face with his fists."

Kerr and three friends stormed out of the house, caught a taxi and headed for his own home. Unfortunately, it was to retrieve a .22-caliber pistol; Kerr "strapped it to his leg in a holster" and returned to the Carroll house. In a scene out of a Western, Kerr stood by the front gate and demanded satisfaction from Lee, who in turn threatened to "stomp his eyeballs out" if he set foot in the house. Lee then said he was "going to apologize" but grabbed an empty beer bottle on his way out of the house and advanced toward Kerr. A witness saw him raise the bottle while five feet away from Kerr and shout, "You're not going to shoot me, Jimmy!" He was. Kerr "fanned" his pistol like a gunslinger, quickly firing four shots into Lee. Kerr then calmly called for a cab to take him home, where the police soon caught up with him.

Kerr was held for a grand jury hearing following an April 2 preliminary hearing. Cross-examination brought out that Lee "had a reputation for assaulting others and was right drunk" that night. However, this would seem to be somewhat counterbalanced by the fact that Lee was shot once in the chest and three times in the back. A circuit court date of October 27 was continued until February 1965 because a key witness didn't show up. According to friends, the young man had "taken off to California" after last being seen in Charlottesville. Kerr's defense attorney expected to get the witness to return in time for the February trial. He apparently succeeded, for in March Kerr pleaded guilty to second-degree murder and was sentenced to eight years in prison, a high price to pay to keep his cigarettes.

"Ha, You Missed!"

Some people always need to have the last word in an argument. In 1965, Glen Irving Clark did get in the last word in a dispute with his former wife, forty-six-year-old Katherine M. Kirk, but it also proved to be the last thing he ever said. Kirk later said that her ex-husband had been harassing her in her home at the Mt. Vernon Trailer Park by "hanging around, banging on the door, throwing rocks, and trying to get in" her trailer. Given that it was reported that they divorced in July 1954, Glen was obviously not one to let the past go. The fact that he was "unemployed and of no fixed address" perhaps sheds some light on the wisdom of Katherine to leave him. Late on November 1, 1965, Clark showed up again, looking for trouble. What happened next was later recounted by neighbor Zemory Short, who was slumbering peacefully until awakened by a gunshot around 11:00 p.m. Looking out his window, he saw Kirk standing outside her trailer with a .22-caliber rifle in hand. "About half a minute" later, two more shots rang out. What direction Clark was walking at the time would prove crucial; initially, Short said Clark was walking away from his ex-wife toward his car, but later he shifted his recollection and said Clark was walking *toward* Kirk.

In her telling, Kirk said that before the shooting, Clark chose the unusual weapon of two license plates and hurled them at her, one cutting her ankle and the other striking her stomach, at which point she opened fire. Clark's response to the fusillade was a prompt retort of "Ha…you missed!" She hadn't. He climbed into his car with a bullet in his left side and began moaning while Kirk went to a neighbor to phone the police. Zemory Short recalled that Kirk commented, "I shot him. Lord, I hope he isn't dead." He was. When speaking to Detective D.C. Whalon, Kirk readily confessed to shooting Clark.

At a February 1966 court appearance, Kirk faced a murder charge and was defended by lawyer Plato Cacheris, who asked that the charges be dismissed on the grounds of self-defense. According to him, Clark "had one of the most extensive criminal records I've ever seen," going back to 1940, including "felonious assault, housebreaking, resisting arrest, and assault on a police officer." Judge John Rothrock declined to dismiss the charges due to Short's initial testimony of Clark walking away when he was shot as well as the fact that Kirk had recently borrowed the rifle from a neighbor, saying that she was going hunting. Presumably this indicated some level of premeditation to Judge Rothrock. However, the grand jury disagreed and in March 1966 declined to issue an indictment. Under the circumstances, it's difficult not to give Kirk the benefit of the doubt when it came to self-defense, and perhaps everyone had to agree, Clark just had it coming.

"I'm Sorry I Did This to You, Baby"

No doubt money has sown more marital discord than almost anything else, but rarely does it end with a husband taking three pistol rounds to the chest. But in 1966 Arlington, that is how one dispute ended. Twenty-six-year-old school bus driver and mother of five Flora H. Dunbar found herself driven to shoot her husband, William, on November 2 in their home at 1315 South Poe Street. Described as a "small, quiet, well-mannered woman" (and in 1966, the newspaper found it necessary to note, "Negro"), Mrs. Dunbar was an unlikely killer.

Things soured in the Dunbar household when twenty-six-year-old William, a post office employee, discovered Flora had a secret checking account. After striking her in the head, he forced her to drive to the bank to deal with the issue, and on their return at about 3:00 p.m., he kicked and dragged her through their front door. (Although it should be noted that the responding police officer apparently did not see any marks or bruises on her.) Pushed inside, Flora ran to the bedroom, where a .32-caliber semiautomatic pistol was kept under their mattress. Warning William to leave her alone, she opened fire when he kept approaching, although the fact that he took one round in the chest and two in the back does make one wonder about the exact circumstances. As William lay bleeding on the floor, Flora later recalled the following bizarre exchange:

Flora: "I'm sorry I did this to you, baby"

William: "That's okay, you told me you were going to do it anyhow."

Flora called an ambulance, and William was taken to Arlington Hospital, where he died that night. As her case was called, Flora became "hysterical," and presumably this condition worsened when word arrived that her husband had died. The charge promptly changed from attempted murder to murder and bond set at $10,000. However, the press evidently lost interest in the story, and it does not appear to have made the papers again. That being the case, it would seem to suggest that the charges were either downgraded or dismissed in what certainly appeared to be a case of self-defense.

Pep Pills Made Him Do It

Described by his father as an "ideal boy in all respects," eighteen-year-old Wiley M. Blevins engaged in some decidedly less than ideal behavior that led to a murder charge in 1967. On February 5 of that year, Blevins had a deadly encounter with Charlie Nicholson, described as "approximately sixty-seven" and a "welfare recipient." Life apparently had not been kind to Nicholson, and the elderly man lived in an abandoned bus behind a grocery store on West Braddock Road owned by Wiley's second cousin, Herschel Blevins, in the logically named Blevinstown area of Fairfax County. Herschel later said Nicholson "drank a little" but never caused trouble.

As Wiley Blevins later told the tale, Nicholson invited him into the woods behind the grocery store to have a beer. Something went very wrong during their drinking session, and an argument developed in which Blevins claimed Nicholson "swore at him" and tried to hit him with his walking stick. Blevins said he knocked him down with his fists, seized the walking stick and proceeded to hit him repeatedly with the cane. Later, Wiley claimed he struck Nicholson only three or four times. A short time later, he walked into his cousin Herschel's store and told him to call the police because there was a dead man in the woods. Herschel not unreasonably assumed he was joking, but Wiley insisted, "I know there is, because I killed him." The police responded following Herschel's call, and the younger Blevins was booked into Fairfax County Jail in lieu of $15,000 bond. Yet another Blevins, this one named Astor, denied any relation to the killer but confirmed that he had also heard him confess. Another witness added that he actually heard Wiley say he "intended to kill 'Honey,'" Nicholson's nickname, but "seemed to be joking." As one could guess by now, this witness was also a Blevins, this time James Alex.

The Blevins family tried to make sense of how Wiley could have done such a thing; Herschel said he was "very sociable" with "no belligerent qualities," and as indicated, his father was likewise shocked by his behavior. Wiley's father laid the blame on "pep pills," saying he had changed his behavior once he started taking them eight months before the murder. Wiley acknowledged being under the influence of the pep pills, as well as beer, when he committed the crime. He eventually made bond and underwent a psychological examination; a grand jury indicted him on May 15. On February 20, 1968, Blevins pleaded guilty to second-degree murder at a non-jury trial. His sentencing was set for April 5, with a potential sentence ranging from twenty years to life. As often happened in cases like this, the media appeared to lose interest in the case, and Wiley's exact sentence was evidently not reported.

THE NAZI PEEPING TOM

A violent and out-of-control youth brought tragedy to a happy suburban family in 1962, shattering the pleasant suburban life led by the Goldfein family in Falls Church. Residing at 1317 Jefferson Avenue (since renumbered), having lived in the neighborhood since 1951, patriarch Solomon Goldfein was a respected chemical engineer employed by Army Materiel Command at Fort Belvoir and an officer at the Fairfax Jewish Center. Wife Marion was a substitute elementary school teacher, and both were originally from New York. Their fourteen-year-old daughter, Sara Lee, attended Falls Church High School, as did seventeen-year-old son Lewis.

The popular Lewis was president of his junior class and was reelected to that position for the newly beginning senior year. He was vice-president of the school student council, a member of the debate team and a player on the varsity baseball and wrestling teams. His physical prowess was evident in an incident that would soon seem portentous; while visiting relatives in New York, he fought off a gang of "young hoodlums" that tried to attack a family member. The bright student, in the top 10 percent of his class, planned to apply to the University of Virginia, MIT, Carnegie Institute and Duke with the intention of becoming a physicist. In short, Lewis Goldfein held seemingly unlimited potential for the future. A small human insight into the boy can be glimpsed when he happened to be quoted in the "Teen" section of a local paper about "What Annoys the Boys on a Date." Amid many amusingly old-fashioned opinions, Lewis offered, "I don't like girls who talk too much and put on a big act."

That September 1, the Goldfeins were playing cards with guests until almost midnight, when the party broke up and the Goldfeins escorted the guests to their car. Lewis commented that it was a clear night and that he should get his telescope. In particular, he wanted to see if a particularly bright star would prove to be Venus or Jupiter. Little could he guess that his decision to remain outside would momentarily have fatal consequences. Lewis set up the small telescope on a charcoal grill about ten feet from the front door and got a metal milk crate to act as a seat. In her upstairs bedroom, sister Sara Lee was getting ready for bed, an incident that apparently served as the catalyst to explosive violence. Even with the venetian blinds drawn, there was a broken slat that allowed someone intent on peeping to look inside her bedroom.

Popular and intelligent high school senior Lewis Goldfein as he appeared shortly before his death. *From the 1962 Falls Church High School Yearbook*

No more than five minutes after Lewis went outside, the quiet night was shattered when father Solomon heard three gunshots outside; Sara Lee thought pebbles were being thrown against her window. Neighbors variously reported hearing between three and five shots. Rushing outside, Solomon looked around his yard and heard Lewis say, "Dad, help me." Looking toward the voice, he found his son lying face down in the backyard with blood pouring from his mouth. As Solomon lifted him up, a spent bullet fell from his shirt; it was the fatal round that punched through his back near the right shoulder and through his right lung, rupturing his pulmonary artery. The family immediately called an ambulance, and Lewis was transported to Fairfax Hospital, but he was pronounced dead one minute after arriving. (By one account, an odd incident occurred: Lewis was declared dead on arrival, but nurses then discovered he was still alive and doctors tried to save his life for a minute before he succumbed.) Regardless, by about 12:45 a.m., forty-five minutes after the shooting, the promising young man was deceased.

Further examination proved that another round had gone through the front of his left thigh, breaking the bone, and a third round had lodged near his lower spine, entering from the rear. It was thought the first round struck his thigh and as he collapsed he spun around, catching the other two bullets in the back. Later, after examining the spent round that had fallen from his shirt and the other bullets taken from his body, police determined that they were fired by a .38-caliber Smith & Wesson revolver or a similar Spanish-made version. Even before those results were obtained—in fact as soon as the call came in—police already had a suspect in mind.

Police headed to 120 East Rosemary Lane (also renumbered since 1962), a short walk of three blocks from the crime scene, "within two hours of the murder, but were unable to arouse anyone." This was the home of "the first suspect who came to their minds." About 2:00 a.m., police officers rang the doorbell at the house, and then pounded on the door when no one answered. Still not getting a response, a police officer called the home's phone; no one picked up. The officers decided to back off for the time being and see what evidence they could collect. The young man they wanted to speak to was in fact inside that house as they sought to gain entry, having what was undoubtedly a strange and excited conversation with his family.

Despite their person of interest, investigators were thorough and interviewed several men involved in previous peeping Tom incidents. Thirty officers searched the area but found no bullets or footprints, partly because of the "hard, dry ground." According to one of the first newspaper reports, the "entire plainclothes force" was used in the search, as was a metal detector. Although no evidence was found, police saw that a person standing on a rise next to the house would have a good eye-level view of Sara Lee's room. Investigators canvassed a twenty-block area around the Goldfein house, methodically speaking to every resident.

Goldfein set up his telescope by number 1 in front of his house, chased the peeping Tom along the line labeled number 2 and was shot in his backyard by number 3. *From the Northern Virginia Sun.*

Police thought back to a series of frightening incidents that occurred in the neighborhood throughout the previous several months. On March 21, a series of sniping incidents occurred; the homes of the Blatt, Barkley and Yong families in the "immediate vicinity" of the Goldfein home had windows shattered by .22-caliber bullets. The nearby Turockzy house then had a brick thrown through a window. The disgruntled Mr. Turockzy grabbed his own gun, pursued a fleeing man he saw and fired five or six times as the suspect fled. Police later said that they questioned several suspects and nothing similar had happened subsequently, so they presumed that they had talked to the person involved and scared him away from repeating his sniping activities. In fact, the night of the shootings, the police encountered a young man already known to them strolling the neighborhood streets with a .22 rifle: John Carroll Vinson Jr., age seventeen. Not surprisingly, he was driven to the police station and questioned, but rather incredibly he was released and the case was never followed up on. Vinson was also questioned about a series of peeping Tom incidents that had been reported that month. Police held on to the rifle, presumably for ballistics testing, but later cited a lack of evidence as the reason they never prosecuted the case. It was never made clear if any testing was in fact done, and one gets the impression the police

The Goldfein house still stands in a quiet neighborhood, with most passersby unaware of the tragedy that occurred there. *Author's collection.*

were satisfied with getting the gun off the streets and giving the young man a stern talking-to. In a few months' time, they would regret that decision, for Vinson was the young man they instantly thought of following Goldfein's murder and it was he who they were seeking on Rosemary Lane. As for the rifle, John never returned to pick it up; apparently, he decided it was best to keep his distance from the police. Anyway, he knew exactly where he could get another gun.

Police returned to Rosemary Lane later on the morning after the shooting, and this time they did make contact with the Vinson family. Mr. and Mrs. Vinson insisted that John was at home at the time of the shootings. The family turned over three .38-caliber pistols for testing; one was his father's service pistol, as he was a police officer in D.C.'s Metropolitan Police Department. The other two were bought by Vinson Jr. One report stated that the pistols were confiscated by Vinson Sr. when he found them in John's possession, but another stated that the younger Vinson actually gave his mother and father one pistol each as a present. It's not hard to imagine that the various members of the Vinson family had reasons to obscure the origins of the guns in the house. However, once the test results came back, none of the guns could be linked to the bullets that killed Lewis. That did not shake the police's belief that they were on the right track with the young John Vinson. Police departed the Vinson house with plans to talk to him again later.

Police also ventured to Alexandria Hospital to interview a woman who had just given birth to her second child, and she had quite a story to tell. On July 9, two months before the shooting, she lived a quarter mile away from the Goldfeins with her husband and two-year-old son in a one-story home on Arlington Boulevard. Her husband was a professional singer and was away on tour that day. After reading until late into the night, she fell asleep with the lights on and blinds open until she awoke around 2:30 a.m. after hearing a banging noise, followed by the sound of the light in her son's room clicking on and off. Thinking the child was just playing around and making the noises, she dozed off again but soon jolted awake when she became aware of a presence next to her. A man loomed over her, and as he reached to touch her, she screamed. He drew his revolver and told her if she stopped screaming she wouldn't be hurt, but she continued her screaming. Unnerved, the man pulled away and discharged a round into the floor, the bullet ultimately lodging in the family piano in the basement. She of course called the police, who determined that the intruder had torn the screen of a back window, reached in and opened the back door. She described the prowler as young with dark hair, over six feet tall, thin and, rather unflatteringly, "kind of pasty-looking." Investigators at her hospital bedside must have exchanged knowing looks; that sounded a lot like John Carroll Vinson.

Little seems to have come from the breaking-and-entering investigation at the time, although police must certainly have thought of their sniping suspect from March. It is not clear why Vinson was not questioned about the July break-in given that he should have been on their radar from the March snipings. Regardless, in September there was no doubt in their minds that Vinson had been the perpetrator both in the break-in and the Goldfein murder. Police had recovered and preserved the round fired that July night and now compared it to the rounds from the Goldfein murder; while it was too damaged to conclusively link to a specific gun, it proved to be a round for a .38 Smith & Wesson, the same type as used in the Goldfein killing.

Meanwhile, over three hundred people attended Goldfein's open-casket memorial service before the interment at King David Cemetery in Arlington. Attesting to the boy's popularity, one of the newspaper reporters at the funeral related that in attendance were "as many teen-agers present as adults, as many Christians as Jews." Throughout the funeral service, plainclothes officers were in attendance to observe anyone looking suspicious. A scholarship fund was soon set up in Lewis's name at Falls Church High School, with donations coming at school, through the mail and from neighbors. Much less appealingly, it was found necessary to station a policeman at the Goldfein house to answer all of their phone calls after the family began receiving "coarse 'crank' calls about their son's death," according to the local paper.

While they may have had strong suspicions about John Vinson, the police had little hard evidence until a stroll through the woods blew the case open. Sterling E. Springston of 1115 Carlton Avenue had lately been taking frequent walks through some woods behind his house. That June, in a strange incident, two teenagers held down his nine-year-old son and the son's eight-year-old friend in those woods and proceeded to burn the boys on their arms with cigarettes. Mr. Springston evidently hoped to find the teenagers loitering in the woods and presumably dispense some justice on them. That is why around 3:30 p.m. on September 3, he was patrolling the woods with his three sons. Glancing down, he saw something sticking out from under a log. Bending down, he saw that it was the handle of a pistol. Thinking quickly, he connected it to the Goldfein shooting and picked it up with a "tobacco pouch" so as not to put fingerprints on it, stripped off his T-shirt and wrapped up the pistol in the shirt. Springston handed the weapon over to police, who placed a dummy in its place and staked out the site to see if the perpetrator returned, to no avail.

Meanwhile, the FBI conducted ballistics testing, comparing the bullet recovered from Goldfein's thigh with the newly recovered gun; it was a solid match. Investigators called Smith & Wesson in Springfield, Massachusetts, and the gun was quickly traced by its serial number to a wholesaler in Rockville, Maryland. In turn, the gun was sold to the Small Arms of the World gun shop in Annandale. There, on June 8, one "John William Vincent" purchased the sixty-five-dollar gun. The store clerk "demanded an affidavit" saying Vinson was old enough (state law in Virginia at the time required the purchaser to be at least eighteen); the buyer complied and said he was a twenty-three-year-old Arlington resident and gave what proved to be a fake address. Having done what the law required of him, the clerk sold "Mr. Vincent" the pistol.

Without naming Vincent, police began to let the public know that they had a suspect. Police Chief William Durrer revealed that a youth was questioned extensively soon after the murder. Chief Durrer also publicly linked the March sniper attacks to the current suspect. Once it became clear that they had the murder weapon, investigators had no doubt about who "John William Vincent" really was. Police decided they had enough

Sterling Springston points to where he found the murder weapon as his sons look on. *From the* Northern Virginia Sun.

evidence to charge Vinson; just after midnight on September 4, they took him into custody. (The Fairfax County Board of Supervisors later made an official commendation of the police for solving the case so quickly.) At the station, when asked to take a polygraph, Vinson said, "I'm innocent. What more do you want?" adding that the polygraph was "just a machine and I don't believe in it." Vinson Sr. also insisted his son was innocent until he recognized the false signature on the weapon's sales slip; it was clearly his son's handwriting. Surely the Vinsons already had suspicions; why else would they have been studiously ignoring the police pounding on their door and calling them in the hours immediately after the murder? Just what sort of discussion was happening while the police tried to get their attention? But now, Mr. Vinson turned to his son and advised him to tell the truth.

John agreed, but he insisted on personally typing his statement. In his version of events, Vinson said that at about 11:45 p.m. on August 31, he decided to head out on a walk, unknown to the rest of the family. He prepared himself for his usual nocturnal activities, slipping the loaded .38-caliber pistol and five extra rounds into his pockets along with a pair of leather gloves. Vinson never attempted an explanation of why he equipped himself in this way for a nighttime stroll.

John initially said that he was walking along the street when he saw a girl undressing in an open window, but in another telling of the story he stated that he was cutting through yards, obviously much more indicative of planned mischief. Regardless, after spotting Sara Lee in her upstairs bedroom, he hid behind a fence as he saw the Goldfeins' guests leaving the house; his view of the girl was partially blocked by a tree, so he adjusted his position and moved in closer after crawling under a board fence. He was spotted by Lewis, although Vinson always maintained that he did not know who it was at the time. As Goldfein took up a run and chased him, Vinson fled but could see that Lewis was gaining ground. Goldfein crashed through the family's badminton net set up in the side yard as he pursued the prowler into the back yard. Vinson spun around when he ran up against a fence and bushes, then unleashed five shots. As he continued his flight, he heard a voice call, "Help, help, I'm shot."

In his statement, Vinson added lamely that it "fills me with the deepest regret and I know I can never rectify this deed. I had no intention of killing Lewis Goldfein. I had not seen him for two years, more or less, since I had left school." While having no choice but to admit that he knew Lewis, this would be his refrain throughout the coming years: he had no idea it was the Goldfein house and he had no idea it was Lewis chasing him, a proposition many would find increasingly hard to believe for reasons that soon became apparent. Already trying to quash accusations of premeditation, he stated, "I want no one to think this was intentional."

Continuing his tale, Vinson said he hid the gun in some woods at the end of Custis Parkway, seventy-five yards from his own house, shoving it underneath a log with the five extra rounds. He gave slightly different versions of where he disposed of the leather gloves, but evidently they were never located. Returning home, he woke up his father in an attempt to establish an alibi, saying he had heard a prowler. John then made what he described as a "feeble attempt" to act out a pursuit of the phantom prowler after arming himself with a sledgehammer. After this odd charade, he took the remaining pistol rounds he had in the house, put them in a paper bag and hid them in the ceiling of an unfinished basement bathroom.

With their suspect now in custody, police began to probe the background of the strange youth. At some point, Vinson had been a gas station attendant but was evidently unemployed at the time of the shootings, raising questions as to how he obtained the money for his gun purchases. Vinson Sr. was a twenty-three-year veteran of the Metropolitan Police in Washington, D.C., but one can infer he did not have a stellar career, as he apparently was still a private and was currently an instructor at the police's traffic violator's school program.

Police pulled out the records of Vinson's past encounters with the law; they were quite recent. He first entered police records on January 3, 1959, when he was reported as a runaway. Evidently, he returned home, for he was soon facing charges of auto theft, tampering and being a peeping Tom. The car-stealing incident occurred in April 1960; after stealing the vehicle, he

An unbothered-looking John Carroll Vinson Jr. (*on the left*) is placed under arrest and escorted by a detective. *From the* Northern Virginia Sun.

was pursued by a police cruiser. Arming himself with a carton of milk, he leaned out the window and threw it on the windshield of the police car. His milk-abetted escape attempt failed, however, although he only received probation for the misadventure. In November of that year, he was charged with a peeping incident, but his probation was simply continued without further punishment or intervention. March brought the sniping incidents described earlier. During that round of questioning, he admitted to over one hundred peeping incidents but wouldn't give police times or places.

On July 29, 1961, he was arrested for vandalizing the car and garage of a doctor in his neighborhood, defacing them with prominent swastikas. This incident and its fallout would put Vinson's shooting of Lewis Goldfein in a very different light. The doctor was Jewish and happened to be the Goldfeins' family doctor. John's past behavior led the police to make contact with him, and he was questioned for hours. Mr. and Mrs. Vinson were apparently away from home at the time, and it's unclear how they reacted to this and John's other criminal activities. By this point, he was receiving outpatient counseling at the Fairfax County Child Guidance Clinic, and the staff there recommended that his probation just be continued. Rather incredibly, the court agreed. Keep in mind that three weeks before the swastika incident, he had escalated his behavior with his July 9 breaking and entering. If ever there was an example of a systematic failure, this was it.

Evidence emerged that Vinson was a fan of George Lincoln Rockwell, leader of the American Nazi Party, and had tried to join the organization. While on trial, Vinson adopted Rockwell's affectations of a pipe and suit. *Library of Congress.*

One investigator of the swastika incident recalled that he "smoked a lot, quoted philosophy and said he was writing a book." Vinson blamed his tired appearance on the fact that he was staying up nights to complete his book. Moreover, he revealed that the swastikas were a deliberate message. As one investigator said, Vinson "hated Jews. I understand he tried to join Rockwell's Nazis." George Lincoln Rockwell was the head of the American Nazi Party, headquartered in nearby Arlington. (In 1968, the American Fuhrer himself was shot to death in a strip mall parking lot by a disgruntled former member of his organization, but that is another story entirely.) A probation official added that John had "exhibited some American Nazi Party literature on one occasion and…once tried to join the organization but was turned down because he was too young."

Here emerged a central issue of the case: was his shooting of Lewis truly random, or did he approach the Goldfein house looking to cause some trouble with a Jewish family? Certainly, he could not have known that Lewis would be outside, so it could not be called a premeditated murder, but perhaps he was targeting the family to see what sort of trouble he could raise. Clearly, he had enough knowledge of the neighborhood to pick out the Jewish doctor in his swastika vandalism, and presumably he gained a great deal of information about the neighborhood through his various prowling and peeping adventures. It behooved Vinson to make the shooting seem random, a panicked response rather than the product of someone looking to cause some trouble with a Jewish family.

In exploring Vinson's background, one reporter noted, the "surprising thing about John Vinson, Jr., is that so few people who knew him were surprised" when he was arrested. Neighbors had plenty to say about the young man: "I suspected it might have been John"; he was "was very polite—too polite, in fact. No 17-year-old acts like that"; "[you] only had to look at him to know he's all mixed up. You couldn't help but notice." And for what it was worth, another neighbor said John was "always playing with matches" as a young child. It was the same old story that so often emerges after a youthful tragedy: though neighbors and family friends thought John was odd, they didn't do anything because they "didn't have anything to go on" and they "didn't want to hurt the parents' feelings."

Adding a bit to the enigma that was Vinson, a family friend recalled one strange occasion when John went with his "deeply religious" mother to a Bible study at a neighbor's house and in "a brief but spirited outburst, he argued the atheist point of view, upsetting the ladies present" and causing his mother to exclaim in considerable embarrassment, "Oh, John!" Still, the friend said he was "not a bad boy, but just not all there." Other acquaintances said he was "moody and exhilarated by turns and much given to the reading of poetry and occasionally to the writing of it" and that the "stuff he wrote was way out." Vinson himself told police that he wrote "weird" poetry. Through his various brushes with the law, officials were equally disturbed by Vinson. After the swastika incident, an assistant commonwealth's attorney was unnerved after meeting Vinson, saying that it "would scare you to talk to him. He looks right through you."

School records did not "indicate that he applied himself in his scholastic work," and he dropped out of Falls Church High School in ninth grade on March 15, 1960. The media soon obtained his school records and found that his "intelligence test scores were above average, but his grades were not," and he suffered the indignity of local papers reporting his final report card: Fs in English and algebra, a D in world geography and a B in general science. His principal said, "Everybody felt he had quite a bit of ability but he certainly did not work up to capacity" and added rather cryptically that his "adjustment in school was not completely satisfactory." Newspaper accounts liked to say that he had an IQ of 165, but it's unclear what the source for this number was. Probably more realistically, his defense attorney later said that he was "above normal intelligence by more than a little bit, but certainly not the genius the early stories made him." John was described as "tall, gaunt, nervous, a chain smoker" but had a "large vocabulary, spoke articulately, was widely read and talked of writing a book at the age of 16." An investigator who interviewed him at the time later said that John had "familiarity with many of the world's great philosophies."

Following the swastika incident, that August his father dispatched him to Eastern State Hospital, a psychiatric institution in Williamsburg. His troubles only escalated in Williamsburg; on August 19, two days after arriving, he and nineteen-year-old Randall Louis Coakley Jr. tied their bedsheets into a rope and lowered themselves out of their second-floor rooms. Hailing cabbie Worley B. Edwards, they robbed him of $41.75 at knifepoint (apparently Eastern State security procedures were not the best) and then attempted to force him into the taxi's trunk before driving off toward Richmond. Police did not have much trouble tracking down a taxi, and the escapees were in custody within two hours.

Vinson was then sent to Southwestern State Hospital in Marion, the maximum-security psychiatric institution in Virginia. His pending warrants from York County followed him to the hospital, intending to charge him with kidnapping, armed robbery and auto theft; however, they were never acted on. In yet another failure of the system, the warrants had been sent from York County to be served and were in his file at Southwestern. However, the superintendent there said he thought they were invalid because a York County judge told him no charges were pending after hospital staff called to check the status of the warrants. As a result, when Southwestern declared him sane, he was released under orders of the Fairfax County Juvenile Court and sent home. After returning from Southwestern State, he continued his weekly outpatient psychiatric care at Fairfax County Child Guidance Clinic, and although it became apparent to all that "he was not capable of living in the community," there was no appropriate institution in which to place him. This, then, is the sad pathway that led a troubled young man to commit an act of explosive violence on that September 1 night.

As the story was picked up by newspapers throughout the country, they tended to focus on Vinson's Nazi inclinations. A Jewish newspaper in Detroit not surprisingly made explicit that it saw the "peeping Tom" claim as a screen for the real cause of Vinson's Nazi fantasies. It further claimed that a "fad among Arlington and Fairfax County youths is to go 'kike-shooting' in the countryside," explaining that "kike" dummies were used for target practice. No doubt anti-Semitism existed in Fairfax County, but Lewis's popularity at school would certainly present another side to the story. A rather tasteless take on the murder appeared in an ad found in a local periodical for *Official Detective Stories—The Peeping Tom Slayer!* Readers were informed that "whoever shot and killed young Lewis Goldfein had no apparent motive—until police started looking for a Peeping Tom! Learn how the alleged killer was brought to justice in the January issue."

Vinson (and at least one other killer in this book) was committed for mental observation at the Southwestern State Hospital in Marion. *Author's collection.*

Events progressed quickly with Vinson in custody. Commonwealth's Attorney Robert C. Fitzgerald (who figures in another story in this book) successfully argued that Vinson should be tried as an adult. The judge agreed, saying that Vinson would be tried as an adult due to the "seriousness of the crime and the maturity of the defendant," referring to the fact that he would be eighteen in about six months and, presumably, his level of intelligence as well. The Fairfax County Juvenile Court waived its jurisdiction, despite defense attorney Philip Brophy's unsurprising opposition. Brophy's request that the press be excluded from the legal proceedings was granted by the judge. The three outstanding warrants, which had been featured enough in the news for a reporter to refer to them as "the famous missing ones," were located, and the whole matter laid before the public.

Vinson's grand jury hearing was put on the docket for September 10, and he was indicted at that time. Vinson pleaded not guilty and was sent back to Southwestern State Hospital for mental observation. Defense attorney Brophy wanted a sanity commission to be held but was overruled. As Vinson had presumably been declared sane once by Southwestern, Brophy anticipated a similar result the second time around. Sure enough, Southwestern staff again said he was sane but had a "personality disturbance." Upon his return in late February, a May date was selected for his trial while he remained held on $50,000 bond. To complete the picture of Vinson's mental state, Commonwealth's Attorney Fitzgerald subpoenaed Vinson's records from the Fairfax County Child Guidance Clinic after staff there would not initially release them.

Vinson and lawyer Brophy made a shift in strategy and gave in to the inevitable; at a hearing on May 27, Vinson waived a jury trial and changed his plea to guilty. Having entered his plea, under Virginia law it remained to be determined what degree of murder Vinson would be convicted of. (Defense attorney Brophy said he would prove the crime was murder in the second degree, while Commonwealth's Attorney Ralph Louk said the state would seek a first-degree conviction.) The next day was given over to psychiatrists debating John's mental state. Dr. F. Regis Riesenman, a perennial defense witness in Fairfax County cases, testified that Vinson's "whole thinking process was warped" (difficult to argue with) and he possessed "impaired judgment" (undoubtedly); however, even he had to concede that John knew right from wrong. Presumably in a bid to earn his pay for the defense, Dr. Riesenman engaged in some tortuous logic when he said that the "very fact that he carried a gun was bad because he placed himself in a position where he might have to use it." The

Southwestern State Hospital superintendent testified that Vinson had a "schizoid personality with sociopathic trends" and, though sane, had a "character disturbance" and a "withdrawn and inadequate" personality, statements that are difficult to argue with. The experts probably did shed a certain amount of light on what caused John to develop as he did; it was noted that his father was "passive" and that his mother was overprotective, leaving him without effective discipline or intervention. Over time, "his personality structure worked into hate and hostility," fueled by the appeal of Nazism and his own "violent and sadistic fantasies." He started to peep into windows because of the sense of control it gave him, leading to greater levels of violence. Louk pointed out the obvious, that bringing a loaded gun and gloves showed premeditation for wrongdoing.

In his own defense, speaking in a "deep, baritone" voice, Vinson unconvincingly stated that he "only intended to frighten" Goldfein when he unleashed the five shots and his sole motive in the affair was trying to see a "pretty girl preparing for bed." Reporters seemed to try to outdo one another in describing Vinson's pale features as he testified, referring to him as a "chalky-faced youth" or having a "pallid face the color of wax." A ballistics expert and the county pathologist testified that the placement of three out of five rounds into Goldfein's body in a dark backyard indicated aimed, intentional fire. Judge Albert V. Bryan Jr. pondered the case and on May 28 announced his decision: guilty of first-degree murder. Judge Bryan called Vinson a "spring gun walking around waiting to be let off" that could not be trusted in normal society. John had nothing to say after the verdict. Sentencing was set for June 21; he was facing a minimum of twenty years in prison.

In the meantime, tragedy struck the Goldfeins again on June 5 when mother Marion died suddenly. She was buried in the same plot as Lewis. The cause of death was determined to be a heart attack, and one can easily imagine the effect her son's death had on her own health.

At the sentencing hearing, prosecutor Louk did not seek the death sentence, while Brophy did his best to emphasize Vinson's youth and mental state. Brophy said Vinson was "like a boy crying for help." Judge Bryan handed down his sentence: life in prison, with eligibility for parole in fifteen years. He said he did this "to protect the public"; unfortunately, the public should have been protected from Vinson long before this point. Displaying no emotion, when asked if he had anything to say, John simply replied, "No, your honor, I have nothing to say."

The Goldfein murdered prompted calls for stricter gun laws in Fairfax County, and debate over a proposed ordinance followed, with not a great deal changing in the end. One positive did emerge from the murder, as calls increased for a youth residential treatment center. The plan came to fruition in November 1963, when the board authorized and provided funds for an adolescent treatment center for youths with issues not severe enough to be institutionalized but who needed help. The end result, called Fairfax House, was a resident treatment center for boys that opened in July 1967, and an article from that time explicitly linked the Goldfein case as a cause for the creation of the institution. Four more houses were proposed, including some for girls. The last mention of Goldfein's murder seems to be when it was discussed in a ten-year newspaper retrospective, and then it disappeared from public view, locked only in the memories of those who knew Lewis.

As for John Carroll Vinson Jr., life in prison ended up meaning just that. Virginia parole records show consistent parole denials for Vinson, with the last coming in December 2020 when John was seventy-five. The reasons given for his parole denial include: "extensive criminal record," "history of violence" and "the Board considers you to be a risk to the community." It is difficult to argue with any of these lines of reasoning. This author began researching the case a number of months later, and by that time, Vinson was no longer listed as an inmate, nor did he appear in any further parole lists. Apparently, he most likely died, still an inmate, sometime in 2021, having served fifty-nine years, a wasted life that destroyed a promising young man along the way.

6
BILLY AND SKIP

Vou are just a few minutes too late, Mrs. Wharton. It just happened."
The caller must have been dumbfounded; she had just desperately dialed the Alexandria Police headquarters to warn them of a murder about to occur. It was no use; a man was dead, and his wife critically injured with an ice pick stuck in her neck. It would not take long for the story to be revealed, and the perpetrator proved to be someone very close to the victim.

Fifty-year-old Donald Cooley resided at 304 East Taylor Run Parkway in Alexandria with his forty-seven-year-old wife, Catherine, and sixteen-year-old stepson William "Billy" Bodmer. Mr. and Mrs. Cooley had been married for eleven years following the death of Catherine's first husband, Elmer Bodmer. Both of the Cooleys taught at Mount Vernon High School, with Donald teaching government and Catherine teaching English. Both were known as well-liked and highly respected teachers who had been at the school for ten years. Billy, soon to begin his junior year, should have attended Hammond High School based on where he lived but was allowed to attend Mount Vernon since his parents taught there. The Cooleys' desire to keep an eye on Billy would have great implications in the near future, but to outside observers Billy seemed to be a generally happy high school student who played on the junior varsity football team. He was described as a "quiet, fair-haired, crew-cut youth who stammers when excited and is troubled with pimples." He was a "good, average" student who spent an extra hour at school each day with parents. Billy also had plans for the future, having written to his senator about obtaining a Naval Academy appointment. If he could not go to the Naval Academy, he was interested in attending Michigan State University. He also planned to attend a boys' summer camp in the coming weeks. The family also included his twenty-one-year-old brother, Jim, who married and moved out in November 1961. At some point, Billy became friends with nineteen-year-old Malcolm L. "Skip" Ward, a part-time shoe salesman who took summer school classes at George Washington High School. The exact nature of their friendship would be examined to a degree that few people could have imagined before July 1962.

Everything changed for the Cooley family on Monday, July 2, 1962. The events of that day were dissected and examined in detail for the next several years, each person with their own version to tell. On that day, in the midst of Billy's summer break, he ran an errand for his stepfather to buy some paint at the local hardware store. Ominously, he made another purchase while there: an ice pick with a four-inch blade. Billy arrived home around 3:00 p.m., but his parents were not there. He ate supper and then went to the Wards' house, returning just after 8:00 p.m. Skip arrived with him in order

Left: Popular teacher Donald Cooley was brutally murdered by his stepson Billy Bodmer; Malcolm "Skip" Ward's involvement in his death was much murkier. *From the* Northern Virginia Sun.

Right: Catherine Cooley, Billy's mother, barely escaped with her life at his hands and had to endure the subsequent trial. *From the* Northern Virginia Sun.

to borrow a .22 rifle for a family trip scheduled to occur in a few days. About 8:10 p.m., Billy asked his mother to borrow his older brother's rifle, went upstairs to get it and handed it to Ward. Catherine was ironing and watching TV and could see what was happening in the living room, where the boys sat and watched TV after they came out of Billy's bedroom. Skip had the .22 rifle casually lying across his lap. A sound similar to firecrackers erupted outside, and Mrs. Cooley stepped into the yard to see what was going on. As she left, Billy got up. He was ready to act.

Mr. Cooley was asleep in his recliner when Billy stood over him, pulled out his recently purchased ice pick and plunged it into his stepfather's torso. A confused Mr. Cooley exclaimed, "What did I do?" as he rose from his easy chair. Mrs. Cooley heard the commotion and came back into the living room to investigate, hurried on by Billy's exclamation to "come quick, Daddy's real sick." As she entered the room, it felt as though Billy slapped her on her back; in fact, Billy stabbed her with the ice pick. However, her attention was focused on Mr. Cooley. She tried to help him toward their bedroom, but he collapsed; when she leaned over to aid him, Billy plunged the ice pick into her back twice more and then jammed it into her neck, where the four-inch blade broke off and stuck. Billy ran into the kitchen and retrieved a butcher knife and continued his frenzied attack on the heavily bleeding Mr. Cooley. It was eventually determined that he stabbed the ice pick and butcher knife into his stepfather's upper body fourteen times. Mr. Cooley staggered into the kitchen, where Skip shot him in the stomach with the rifle, the bullet lodging in his left kidney. Like much of what occurred in those few moments, the circumstances of that shot would be hotly debated. In the confusion and stress of the moment, Catherine was still unaware that she had been stabbed. She had the presence of mind to call a doctor, who quickly placed a call to the police. Upon the arrival of the police and an ambulance, Mr. Cooley was found covered in blood but still clinging to life. The ambulance rushed Cooley to Alexandria Hospital, but he died an hour after arriving.

An alert was issued to be on the lookout for the two youths, and early on the morning of July 3, Baltimore police found Billy Bodmer sleeping in a 1957 blue and white Ford, which would become the source of much controversy. Arrested about 3:30 a.m. at a gas station in the Cherry Hill neighborhood, Billy had blood on his shirt but was unarmed. He waived extradition (although how much would a teenager really have known about what that meant?), and the Alexandria police came to pick him up. Baltimore police relayed that he was "not a bit remorseful" and told police that he expected to spend a few years in juvenile detention before being released. As for his mother, she would be taken care of by Cooley's insurance. However, the façade evidently didn't last long and Billy "broke down" under questioning and sobbed, "Tell my mother I'm sorry….I hope she gets along all right." Statements were taken by both the Baltimore and Alexandria police, and both confessions would be used in court.

It did not take long to track down Skip; he was arrested at his home at 9:15 p.m., just an hour or so after the murder. In fact, Alexandria police private Jerry Shockley was waiting for Ward when he returned to his family home. Ward explained that he left the Cooley house in their family car with Bodmer at the wheel, but he told Billy he wanted to go home, so Billy stopped at the Shirley Duke Apartments to let him out. Later, information would come out that brought into question Ward's telling of that drive. Ward's father said Skip came home "in a bad state of shock" and said he'd seen "a terrible tragedy." Ward's parents protested the police questioning him and evidently were vociferous enough that Shockley threatened to arrest them, but Shockley always insisted that Ward talked to him willingly in the police car, where he "freely described the murder" and was "completely candid." While talking to Shockley, Ward exclaimed, "God! I saw a terrible thing!"

On July 16, Billy and his mother, released from the hospital on July 9, appeared at the Alexandria Juvenile Court. Mrs. Cooley was unable to attend her husband's funeral in Berryville, Virginia, due to her hospital stay. In court that day, Billy was "certified" as an adult to the Corporation Court, which assumed jurisdiction in a hearing "marked by tearful breakdowns by the mother." Billy "sat quietly" until the end of the hearing and then burst into tears when embraced by his grandmother. The Corporation Court would decide if Billy would be tried as an adult; he was held for a September 13 grand jury, where indictments for the murder of his stepfather and felonious assault on his mother were filed. By then, Bodmer was represented by attorney William P. Woolls Jr., and before Billy entered a plea Woolls filed a motion questioning the court's jurisdiction and asked that the indictments be dismissed, adding, "I don't think the preliminary hearing was in accord with the law." Judge Franklin P. Backus denied the motions but agreed to postpone the arraignment hearing. Woolls proved to be correct, for on October 10, he successfully argued that the September 13 grand jury was "illegally constituted" because one of the five grand jurors was a Fairfax County resident, not an Alexandria resident. As a result, a new grand jury was to be called later in the week, although Commonwealth's Attorney Earl F. Wagner wanted one called immediately, accusing Woolls of

Malcolm "Skip" Ward is shown soon after his arrest, the beginning of a long legal odyssey. *From the* Northern Virginia Sun.

using "dilatory tactics." A defiant Woolls responded that he might just enter new motions as well. Woolls was not successful in getting Billy released on bail and he remained in jail, even though his mother was willing to take him back in.

Bodmer's respite from the indictment was brief, as he was reindicted by the new grand jury on October 13. Bodmer entered a not guilty plea, with the trial set for November 19. Since by this time Ward had also already entered a not guilty plea, his right to have his indictments quashed was waived. Ward, likewise charged with murder and felonious assault, was scheduled for trial on November 29. Wagner intended to try Bodmer first, even if it would delay Skip Ward's trial, set for November 29. Bodmer's trial date was delayed for a psychiatric examination, and it became clear that Woolls intended to raise the issue of sanity; the exam was expected to take two weeks. His trial was eventually scheduled for February, while Ward's trial was also delayed until

March 25. T. Brooke Howard, Ward's attorney, requested a jury trial, yet it was anticipated that Bodmer's trial would not have a jury.

In the second week of February 1963, Bodmer changed his plea to guilty, and Judge Backus postponed sentencing pending a background report from the county probation office. Under Virginia law, it remained for Judge Backus to decide if it would be a first- or second-degree murder conviction. At the hearing several days later, Judge Backus heard three hours of testimony from the prosecution and no testimony or witnesses from the defense, although "dozens of relatives and friends" of Bodmer were present at the hearing. The defense tried to bar Billy's two confessions as being improperly obtained, but Backus allowed them as evidence. The biggest revelation proved to be Billy's motive in the murder. In the Baltimore confession, Bodmer said he was "tired and fed-up of being embarrassed" by his stepfather in front of his friends and added that his parents were strict and did not give him "privileges the other kids had," like using the family car, swimming and staying out late in the summer and non-school nights. He "felt family restrictions over the hours he could stay out and his use of the family car were too strict, and his life was hemmed in many other ways." The family car seemed to be central to Billy's growing rage. Bodmer said there had been issues over privileges ever since Cooley became his stepfather, but Catherine Cooley insisted that there had never been signs of resentment from Billy and he never complained about not being able to use the car. He could ask to use it if he had a specific reason and, in fact, had been allowed to use it the weekend before the murder to go to a party. However, Mrs. Cooley also described Billy as a shy, "pitiful" boy and, somewhat in contradiction to her earlier statement, said he openly stated that he "hated his stepfather's guts." One gets the impression that Billy was too timid or nonconfrontational to fully address his issues with his stepfather and the internalized resentment continued to build, with disastrous results.

Given Billy's description of his stepfather as overbearing, it should be noted that Mr. Cooley's principal Melvin Landes stated that he was "very popular" with his students, with Landes stressing the word *very*. Likewise, Mrs. Cooley was "well respected and considered one of the best teachers on the staff." The fact that both were sponsors of school clubs and Mrs. Cooley was a class sponsor seems to support that they were popular with students. Principal Landes added that in his thirty years of working with students he had "never run into anything as mystifying as this." Perhaps reflecting a more innocent time, Landes added, "They say money is the root of all evil. I say cars are the root of all evil around the high school." A

Ward became very familiar with the courtroom that was then located inside Alexandria City Hall. *Library of Congress.*

warm tribute in the school's yearbook echoed the positive comments about Mr. Cooley, describing him as "extremely well liked," a "gentleman" and a teacher "who gave unselfishly of his time to student government work and other student activities."

A neighbor added to the portrait of Bodmer and said that Billy had to be on his best behavior and not do anything that would reflect on his parents as teachers, which was a "handicap to him." Others testified that his parents were strict but the family "appeared congenial at school." His algebra teacher and coach John Miller said he was a "very nice boy, well mannered, quiet....I was really shocked." Other observations about Billy were more nuanced, with one neighbor noting that he would "turn red in the face when you'd speak to him" due to his stutter, and another said he "always had his head in a book." In later legal proceedings, Keith Lyman, a friend of Skip's, said he heard Bodmer say he hated his parents, and Ernest Edward Murphy Jr., Skip's second cousin, had more alarming testimony when he said that he saw Billy pick up a letter opener and say, "This should do for my ol' man." Skip's great-uncle Edward Murphy Sr. added he heard Billy say he hated his stepfather, and when he asked him why, Billy said he wanted a father like Skip's and that Cooley was too strict. Murphy claimed he "lectured the boy on the essentials of the Fourth Commandment"; if he did, the lesson obviously didn't work. Regardless of what others thought of Billy, a court-ordered mental exam from Alexandria psychiatrist Elmer F. Lowry confirmed that he was mentally competent and at the time knew right from wrong and was not under an "irresistible impulse" to commit the murder.

There was one incident that perhaps contributed to the explosion of violence. Although generally described as a well-behaved boy, on June 2, a month before the murder, Billy was "put on restriction" by his mother because he set off a fire extinguisher at McArthur School in their neighborhood, presumably as some sort of prank. During his "restricted" period, he called Ward and told him to come see him while he was grounded since he couldn't leave the house. What exactly the two discussed over those weeks would differ sharply as they each told their side of the story in court.

As emerged from the court appearances and statements thus far, Billy started planning his parents' deaths after Christmas 1961 and first considered putting arsenic in his stepfather's food and then actually put lye into Mr. Cooley's evening drink of whiskey, but he spat it out and it only "made him woozy." According to Commonwealth's Attorney Earl F. Wagner at the initial hearing, "Things reached the boiling point at the end of school in June." Perhaps the fact that the family was now spending all day together during the summer break ratcheted up the tension inside Billy. That month, Bodmer was driving back from Loudoun County with his parents and considered grabbing the wheel to wreck the car but "lost his nerve." He then considered killing them with their gas stove, according to Wagner, but Billy interjected with a shout of "That's not so!" when that claim was made. Bodmer admitted that he and Ward "planned it all week" but claimed that "I didn't know whether I could go through with it or not." Allegedly, he called a friend on the morning of the murder and told them about the planned attack, saying it was planned for 3:00 p.m., after his parents had cashed their paychecks. He resolved to stab whichever of his parents came home first but lost his nerve when his mother entered the house. After his stepfather came home and took a shower, Billy then decided to use a fireplace poker as a weapon but again could not go through with it. In the time just before the murder, Billy spent a final few minutes "deciding if I should or not.…I then plunged the ice pick into my father, aiming at the heart."

Billy apparently did not keep his plans secret. According to one friend, Bodmer talked about killing his parents for two months and had "often discussed the relative 'merits' of different sharp instruments." A fellow student said Bodmer told him he put sleeping pills in Cooley's coffee so that he could use the car, and another said he picked up a letter opener and said, "This would be good to use on my old man." In testimony that had future consequences, Skip's eighteen-year-old brother, Michael "Timmy," testified that Billy talked "constantly" about murdering his stepfather and that while he liked his mother, he'd have to kill her too because "she'd tell on him."

However, Timmy Ward added that Billy always said it in a "joking manner" and "I never believed he'd do it." Ward acknowledged that the brothers discussed Billy's plans, but Timmy told him not to pay attention to Billy because he had been talking about killing his parents for a long time and was "trying to be big."

After hearing and considering the testimony, it did not take Backus long to determine that Billy was guilty of first-degree murder. Almost as an afterthought, on March 1, Bodmer appeared in court to plead guilty to felonious assault on his mother in a hearing that took less than two minutes. While there were certainly attempts by Bodmer to blame Ward for influencing him toward killing his parents, the full dispute about Ward's level of involvement had not yet begun.

Meanwhile, following Ward's arrest, he was held for grand jury action, and his initial hearing was "marked by heated exchanges" between Earl Wagner and defense attorney T. Brooke Howard. Arguing over the issue of bond, Wagner referred to Howard's "good showmanship," and "Howard heatedly returned that and other compliments." Ward pleaded not guilty, and his trial began on March 25. It would prove to only be the first step in a legal drama that dragged on for the next three years. He faced a jury of ten men and two women; the jury selection had been lengthy because many in the pool already had an opinion about the case, had read too much about it in the papers or were opposed to the death penalty. Wagner asked for death or life in prison. The crux of the issue came down to whether Ward was an accomplice and active participant or an unwitting observer. Bodmer testified for two hours at Ward's trial, "stuttering painfully," and blamed him for instigating the murders. In a moment that had significant implications, Wagner asked Bodmer if he had just been convicted for the murder. Howard "jumped to his feet, objected and moved for a mistrial," but Bodmer was allowed to answer, "Yes." Wagner repeated the testimony in his closing argument over Howard's objection. Howard's argument was that Bodmer's conviction had no bearing on the guilt or innocence of his client and it would inappropriately influence the jury. Billy claimed that it was Ward who offered suggestions on different ways to kill Cooley. Bodmer admitted that he contemplated using a car accident or poison to kill Cooley in December 1961 but claimed that the thought "left my head" until Ward brought it up in June. Bodmer vaguely referred to an argument with his stepfather on the day of the murder but insisted that he was not determined to kill him until he visited Skip after dinner and Ward said that "he would help if I needed help."

According to Bodmer, they discussed the attack in his bedroom, and Ward willingly volunteered to shoot one of the adults while Billy stabbed the other when a signal was given. Specifically, he supposedly offered to shoot Mrs. Cooley "because she might scream" when Billy attacked his stepfather. Bodmer said he lost his nerve, and his mother left the house to investigate the sound of firecrackers. Cooley was sleeping in his chair when Ward waved the ice pick and said, "Now, now is your chance." Bodmer said Ward twice "drew a bead" on Mrs. Cooley as she looked out the window, but he waved him off.

Ward's telling of events not surprisingly differed greatly from Billy's. He acknowledged that Bodmer started talking about killing his parents three weeks before the murder, but he did think Billy was serious. This was somewhat undercut by his admission that Bodmer wanted him to participate in the murder when he coughed as a signal, so presumably he thought that Ward was going along with a plan they had discussed. If Ward truly thought Billy was joking, it seems that he was letting him take the joke very far. However, he insisted that his trip to Billy's house on the night of the murder was simply to borrow the rifle for his upcoming trip.

Ward said Bodmer talked of killing his parents four times that day, but he "shunted it off" and thought his threats were in the vein of someone threatening to run away from home. Skip admitted he called Billy twice on July 2 but said it was only to ask for a ride home. During one call that afternoon, he alleged that Bodmer said, "What's the matter with you?… Don't call me….My mother's asleep on the couch and I'm going to stab her." Skip responded, "Forget about that stuff." When he arrived to borrow the .22 rifle, Ward swore he told him, "Stop talking that nonsense…it'll warp your mind." Ward did admit that when Bodmer brought up stabbing his parents that evening, he said, "I couldn't kill an animal that way, Billy, and if you're going to kill anybody, best use a rifle, a high-powered rifle." Even more damningly, in his first statement to police Ward described this or a similar incident and acknowledged that since Bodmer said he had a gun but no bullets, Ward took him to a friend who gave Billy seven rounds. Billy confirmed that a conversation like this occurred when he told Skip he wanted to use the ice pick, but Ward told him it was quicker to shoot Mr. Cooley; Billy responded, "No, I have an ice pick and I've been sharpening it all morning." Bodmer also said he showed Ward how to load the .22; he cocked it for him and told him, "It's all ready." (However, prosecutors later noted that Skip was a member of the St. Mary's National Rifle Association chapter from May to December 1960, showing he had knowledge of rifles and the association advisor said he "was a good shot.") Billy then put the ice pick under his shirt. According to Skip, the following exchange took place just before the killing:

"I'm going to do it."

"Do what?"

"Stab my father. Mom is outside."

"Are you going to shoot your mother?"

"No, get that thought out of your head."

When the bloodbath began, Skip swore that he stood by as a horrified onlooker.

There was a major problem, however: not even Skip could deny that he had shot Mr. Cooley. Ward insisted that he did not deliberately shoot Cooley; rather, the rifle accidentally went off when he turned to run through the kitchen as the bleeding Mr. Cooley "staggered toward him." As Ward tried to open the door out of the kitchen, a rug jammed underneath it, and as he leaned in with his shoulder to force the door open, the rifle went off. Ward said he did not even remember pulling the trigger. Defense attorney Howard brought the rifle into court in order to demonstrate how it was "accidentally" fired, but it is difficult to imagine a likely position where Ward had managed to turn around the rifle barrel behind him while "accidentally" pulling the trigger. Ward also was unable to explain why he didn't just drop the rifle if he was so intent on fleeing the scene.

More detail was brought out regarding the boys' actions after the murder, as evidently they stopped at the Shirley-Duke Shopping Center drugstore before Skip left the car, which he neglected to include in his original version of events. In his first telling, Skip stated that after the murder Billy told him to get in the car and he told Billy to take him home, which he did. Seventeen-year-old Patricia Weaver told a fuller story when she testified that she was supposed to go on a date with Billy the next night, and she saw the two boys at the drugstore. Evidently, nothing in their behavior alarmed her, and she agreed to give Skip a ride home. The route home took them past the Cooley house, now surrounded by police cars; Ward quickly ducked down below the dashboard but did not explain his strange behavior to Patricia. Obviously, the implication was that Ward was much more likely to have been a willing participant in the crime if he was calmly hanging out with Bodmer at the drugstore moments after the murder.

Ward's fifteen-year-old girlfriend ("former girlfriend" by the time of his trial), Linda Carol Light, testified that he told her on the day of the murder that Ward was planning to kill his parents; when asked in court if she knew when it was to occur, she said, "I guess it was supposed to be between 1 and 3:30." She added that Skip called her around 10:00 a.m. that day and said Billy had finally done it and killed his parents, then said he was only joking. Her reply was simply that "he's about dumb enough to do it." Skip then spent most of the day at her house, from about 12:00 to 5:00 p.m. He was supposed to be home around 5:00 or 5:30 p.m. to help his mother wash windows.

Linda came to the home of Mrs. John L. Wharton (reflective of the times, she suffered the indignity of not even having her own first name published) around 12:45 p.m. to "set Mrs. Wharton's hair" but asked if she could delay the appointment until 4:00 p.m. due to a dental appointment. (This was apparently not quite true, given Linda's testimony that she in fact spent the afternoon with Skip at a swimming pool and then went to her house as stated above.) Mrs. Wharton agreed; when Linda returned, she "seemed worried," and when questioned, she said that Skip related to her a phone conversation he just had with Billy, who said he was going to kill his parents at 9:30 p.m. when they went to bed, then take the bodies to West Virginia and throw them into the Shenandoah River. Over time, Linda gave sharply conflicting accounts of Skip's response: in one version he asked Billy "if he wanted help," and in another he warned Billy that he couldn't get away with it. One can't help but suspect that she shifted her version of the phone call to one more helpful to Skip. Billy had a ready response to Skip's supposed warning: the neighbors knew his parents were planning a trip, and they wouldn't notice them going missing. Over time, Linda also gave different versions of how she responded: either she told Skip not to go to Billy's house or she brushed it off, commenting, "Did you ever hear of anything so ridiculous? You know a person couldn't do anything to their parents like that." Again, a more ominous version seems to have shifted toward one more innocuous.

Mrs. Wharton was understandably concerned, and although she thought it was "far-fetched," to be safe she investigated further. Picking up the phonebook, she and Linda looked for the name Bodmer but came up empty, not knowing that Billy's "father" was in fact his stepfather, named Cooley. Not to be deterred, Mrs. Wharton called the operator, who could not find a listing for Bodmer. Linda then called the Ward house to get the Cooleys' number but evidently "did not explain her purpose, though, and was unable to obtain it," and an "inquiry to Ward's brother also was unproductive." Why Linda did not get on the phone and clarify things was not explained. Eventually, Linda mentioned to Mrs. Wharton that Billy's parents were teachers at Mount Vernon High School; the time this occurred was later put at just after 8:00 p.m., which would suggest that the inquiries may not have been as hurried or desperate as Wharton's and Light's testimony implied, presuming Linda did arrive near the 4:00 p.m. time she planned. Even if Linda waited until the end of the appointment to discuss the matter, there seemingly would have still been a couple of hours to track down the Cooleys' phone number or, for that matter, drive to the Ward house for information. Regardless, finding out that the Cooleys taught at Mount Vernon proved to be a vital piece of information, for Mrs. Wharton worked for the school board and knew the Mount Vernon principal, Mr. Landes. Calling him up, she explained the situation but was told, "I think you are upset for nothing. I know that boy well. He's one of the nicest boys we have and his parents are very nice. You don't have a thing to worry about." Unconvinced, Mrs. Wharton "persisted," and Mr. Landes rather reluctantly gave her the Cooleys' phone number and explained the confusion about their last name. She called, and the phone "rang and rang and rang and there was no answer." Finally, she placed a call to the Alexandria police headquarters, only to be told that it was too late; Mr. Cooley was dead. This of course begs the question of why she did not just call the police in the first place if she suspected a murder was about to happen; again, one can't help but suspect that she or Linda may have embellished the story a bit for dramatic effect.

The nature of Billy and Skip's friendship was also probed. Catherine Cooley said she had known Ward for about four months and seen him twelve or fifteen times and overheard on other occasions when he called Billy. She said the phone calls became much more frequent in the last two weeks of June, sometimes occurring twice a day. Anytime Skip was over, there was always a "cordial atmosphere." Malcolm Ward Sr. testified and said that he met Bodmer through his younger son Timothy around April when he would come over to play pool; they also played sports together. He claimed he didn't know that Bodmer and Skip were spending time together. Timmy Ward said Skip had once asked him if he thought Billy would really hurt his parents, and Timmy said no. He agreed with his parents that Billy was his friend, not Skip's, and they were "extremely close." Timmy insisted that he had never seen Billy and Skip together outside of the Ward house. Ward's former girlfriend Linda offered her take on the relationship, saying that in the time she had been dating Skip since April 1962, she had not met Bodmer until the night of the junior-senior prom in June and then had seen him three more times. She acknowledged that she spent enough time with him to know that he had access to a car and to recognize his voice.

After four days of testimony and a visit by the jury to the Cooley house, closing arguments began on March 28. Howard said everything came down to whether the jury believed Ward or Bodmer. He acknowledged that Ward showed "no judgment whatsoever" and acted "stupidly," but he didn't think that Bodmer was serious. For his part, prosecutor Wagner insisted Ward convinced Billy to go through with the murder and "had egged him on" by calling several times and asking him if he'd done it.

After conferring for over six hours with the attorneys, Judge Backus gave the jurors thirty-eight instructions and said they must believe Ward had "malice in his heart" to convict of murder; the other options were involuntary manslaughter or acquittal. The jury retired to deliberate and eventually sent word that they could not reach a verdict after deliberating for four hours and twenty minutes; a mistrial was declared. A new trial was set for April; Ward took the news "impassively," but his mother began to weep. Evidently, there was a fairly even split in opinions, as one juror said it was not "a case of one or two jurors holding out."

Meanwhile, Bodmer's sentencing hearing began on April 9. Friends, teachers, classmates, a minister and a probation officer testified, with the general consensus being that he was a "quiet, retiring, well behaved boy of average intelligence." However, probation officer Hubert A. Hardy said Bodmer was a "withdrawn boy unable to express feelings or aggression" and had a tendency to stammer and stutter under pressure. Dr. Elmer F. Lowry Jr. said his personality was "pretty thoroughgoing squelching and repression for most emotional reactions," and his inability to express his feelings "built up an intensity to the exploding point." More than one witness testified to the effect that his parents expected him to be a "perfect kid," and his sister-in-law Sandra L. Bodmer said Mr. Cooley was very strict and would make "fun of him" about his stutter. After fifteen character witnesses testified, sentencing was deferred until May 14 so that Judge Backus could investigate an offer to send Billy to a rehabilitation center for boys. Reverend Herbert A. Willke of St. James Episcopal Mission said he could be sent to an Episcopal boys' home in Kansas; he had received offers of financial help in sending Billy there.

The sentencing hearing reconvened as scheduled. The plan to send Billy to the rehabilitation home fell through; on learning of the exact circumstances of the case, the home evidently declined to take in Bodmer. Judge Backus did not seem keen on the idea anyway. Backus sentenced Bodmer to forty-eight years for murder and a concurrent four-year sentence for felonious assault on his mother. Backus said that he was not suspending any of the sentence because the murder was "willful, deliberate, and premeditated." Under Virginia law, Billy would be eligible for parole after serving one-quarter of his sentence. Bodmer received the news calmly and silently; as he left the courtroom, he asked a friend to write and said, "I'll write too."

On June 17, Ward's second trial began; he had been free on bond since the first trial. The testimony was largely a repeat of the first trial, and the jury again paid a visit to the crime scene. One new witness was Ward's mother, who said she didn't testify at the first trial because she was under a doctor's care due to stress. She added some intriguing details to the case. She stated that he worked after school and had the use of the car on Saturdays but she could account for his whereabouts every day. On the day of the murder, Bodmer called three times asking for Timmy, then asked if Skip was home from summer school. Skip told his mother that he might go to Billy's house. Mrs. Ward claimed this was the first time the two boys spoke on the phone. She reiterated her husband's claims that Billy and Skip were not well acquainted and that Billy was really Timmy's friend. Wagner then asked an excellent question: Why would Skip go to Billy's house if they were not acquainted? She could only reply, "I don't know. He just said that as he went out the door." In her apparent efforts to cover for her son, she inadvertently hurt his case. According to her, Skip wanted to borrow Billy's .22 rifle to use for target shooting for a July 4 visit to relatives. (Would you really borrow a firearm from a near stranger?) In an important point she evidently didn't pick up on, Mrs. Ward told him that he could use the guns of the relatives they were visiting and didn't need to borrow a gun, but Skip insisted that he wanted to borrow Bodmer's rifle. The implication is that there was no legitimate reason for Skip to borrow the gun for the forthcoming trip, and presumably he had another use for it in mind. As he left that evening, he patted her on the shoulder and said cryptically, "You were always afraid of guns, weren't you, Mom?"

There was also a new wrinkle in the case: Ward's defense planned to subpoena Martin Frickleton, Billy's cellmate, convicted of narcotics possession and escaping jail. He supposedly heard Bodmer say he would offer damaging testimony against Skip in revenge for his brother Timmy testifying against him in his own trial. Bodmer denied the story, and Howard did not call on the convict to testify. Obviously, it was determined that the veracity of his testimony was not strong. Again, the crux of the matter came down to whether Bodmer or Ward was the most believable, so much of the testimony focused on Ward's trustworthiness. On the fourth day of the trial, both sides presented witnesses that gave differing accounts of Ward's honesty. Six neighbors testified to Skip's honesty; however, three teachers and his principal at George Washington High School said his reputation for honesty was "bad" and overall his reputation "could have been better" and was "not very good." Throughout the trial, Skip was "extremely attentive" and at times "seemed to be re-examining Earl Wagner." However, when asked by Wagner why as a nineteen-year-old he didn't call the hospital or get help if he truly hadn't been part of the murder, Ward rather lamely replied, "I did not want to be reminded of what had happened. I wanted to get it out of my mind." Wagner called Ward a "thrill killer" and asked for a forty-year sentence, while Howard said he was simply a "stupid individual" who was a "fall guy." According to Howard, Bodmer "wanted Ward with him from the first….He is not going to be happy unless he has Ward with him" in prison.

On June 21, after nearly six hours of deliberation, at 8:06 p.m. the jury announced its decision: guilty. Skip "pounded his fist against the courtroom bar, his mother wept hysterically, and gasps of surprise resounded through the courtroom." Ward rushed out of the courtroom, and a clerk rushed after him as his mother shouted, "It isn't fair!" and dramatically fainted in the courtroom with an ambulance eventually taking her away. Also upset were "teenage girls who have followed the case from its beginning last October, and who have attended the retrial every day this week"; they "moaned and cried on each other's shoulders" when the decision was announced. Howard moved to set aside the verdict and hearing scheduled for July 9. Not surprisingly, this was denied by Backus, and on the ninth, he sentenced Ward to forty years in prison, with parole eligibility in ten years. When asked if he had anything to say, Skip simply replied, "No sir, it wouldn't do any good." Backus agreed to postpone the start of the sentence and release Ward on bond while Howard decided if he would appeal.

Howard did appeal the case, and the Appeals Court agreed with the request and remanded the case to the Supreme Court of Appeals. As the new year of 1964 began, the Virginia Supreme Court agreed to hear the case. In October, the decision came through: the Virginia Supreme Court overturned Skip's conviction because the jury should not have been allowed to hear Bodmer's testimony that he had just been convicted of murder. Howard's objection was deemed to be correct; according to the decision, "both the question and the statement by the commonwealth attorney were prejudicial to the accused and a mistrial should have been ordered."

Despite Howard's successful efforts, for his third trial in February 1965, Ward retained Robert T.S. Colby and Dikran Kavaljian as his attorneys. Ward's trial had barely begun when, no doubt to everyone's frustration, it emerged that jurors had been reading news accounts of the case. On Colby's request, Judge Backus polled the jury on who had read about the case, and seven members admitted to reading "news reports concerning the latest proceedings" the night before and even that very morning. On February 16, Backus had no choice but to declare a mistrial. A new trial date was set for May 3 while Ward remained free on bond.

Ward's fourth trial began with a jury of ten men and two women. Little new information emerged; Billy, now nineteen, returned to testify, and Ward said it was hard to recall all the details of events because the "first trial sort of got to me." Following the third day of testimony, Judge Backus was taking no chances; he ordered the jurors to be "locked up." In closing arguments, defense attorney Colby admitted that other people might have handled things differently, but Ward was young and "probably not so bright." During jury deliberations, Ward smoked and walked around the courthouse with his arm around a girl, who proved to be his sixteen-year-old fiancée. Skip was a week away from his twenty-second birthday. Two hours after deliberations began, Skip evidently figured he might as well take advantage of being at the courthouse and tried to get a marriage license. The young lovers were accompanied by the girl's mother, but the effort was futile. The clerk said he couldn't issue the license because Ward's fiancée lived in Fairfax County, and she had to get one there. Disappointed, Ward waited while the jury deliberated for nine hours.

Finally, on May 6, the years of legal drama came to a close. The verdict: involuntary manslaughter. The sentence: five years. The eight months Ward spent in jail following his first conviction would count toward his sentence; parole would be possible in fifteen months. His fiancée wept as the judge pronounced the sentence, but Ward just smiled at her and said, "I'll be back" as he was led away. Catherine Cooley returned to teaching and passed away in 1995. After being paroled, Ward married and had three children and evidently lived a quiet life until he died in 2013 at the age of seventy. After his parole, Bodmer worked as a truck driver, married and had two children before he died of leukemia in 2009 at the age of sixty-three. Given that he married in 1971, it would seem likely that parole guidelines changed, as he either married in prison or did not serve the one-quarter sentence he was originally supposed to. Needless to say, Billy Bodmer's obituary made no mention that he once had a stepfather until a far-off, fateful night in 1962.

THE HILLBILLY SINGER'S REVENGE

On a chilly winter night in January 1964, a promising young musician met his death at the hands of a failed musician seized by jealousy. James "Bud" Oliver was born in 1945 in New York City. The Duke University freshman was on a midterm school break and was visiting his family at 2750 Ives Street in Arlington. He planned to depart early on the morning of January 28 for his return to Durham, North Carolina. He had graduated from Wakefield High School the previous year; after playing the clarinet in his high school band and the Arlington Symphony, he continued his musical efforts in the Duke marching band and Duke Symphony. In an eerie parallel with a man about to change his family's life forever, he planned to make music a career. His father, Wayne, was the associate editor of *U.S. News and World Report* and was a rather well-known figure in Washington, D.C. media circles. Before returning to Duke, Oliver arranged a date for January 27 with a girl he had dated a number of times previously, eighteen-year-old Bonnie Bell, a senior at Washington-Lee High School. The pair met through the Arlington Symphony, where Bonnie played the cello and piano. Though they evidently had gone on dates for a year or so and were later described as "very fond" of each other, they apparently were not boyfriend and girlfriend.

The date went off pleasantly, and Oliver drove Bonnie home at about 10:30 p.m. The couple spent a few moments talking in the car, almost directly in front of the Bell house at 717 North Emerson Street. An abrupt knock on the driver's side window startled the pair, and the door flew open. While the man forcing his way into the car was a complete stranger to James,

Bonnie immediately recognized the angry man: James Reymer. The clearly agitated Reymer was brandishing a .38-caliber Smith & Wesson pistol and had a scent of liquor on his breath; Oliver not unreasonably assumed he was being robbed. He told Reymer to take his money if that's what he wanted, but Reymer simply crawled over him and forced himself between the couple before telling Oliver to start driving down Emerson toward 6th Street. Some conversation passed between the three, and Oliver began to grasp the situation.

At some point, he said something to the effect of "Can't you see she doesn't want you anymore?" and according to Bonnie, that sent Reymer into a rage. Reymer quickly became "extremely upset…abusive and unreasonable" and ordered Oliver to stop the car. Announcing, "I want to get this whole thing settled," he climbed into the back seat, turned around and fired two shots into Oliver. He fell across Bonnie's lap, and when it appeared that Oliver tried to rise up, Reymer fired two more shots into him. Medical examiners later found that Oliver was hit once in the head and three times in his body. Reymer climbed into the driver's seat and forced Bonnie to help him shove the dying James into the back, "like he was nothing, a fly he swatted," as Bonnie later put it. At this point, she "didn't know if he was dead or not—it seemed to me he should be." A car pulled up behind them, and Reymer took off driving for a few minutes while he "talked wildly" and threatened Bonnie with his pistol until he stopped in front of her house. Without another word, he got out of the car and walked to his own car, a black 1963 Volkswagen, parked nearby. The shocked teenager drove the "blood-spattered car" ten blocks to Arlington Hospital, but Oliver was dead by the time she arrived at 11:15 p.m. At home, his parents' calendar bore a notation on January 28 that would never be fulfilled: "Bud goes back." The innocent victim was buried in the family cemetery in Wakulla, Florida, where, as a newspaper report sadly noted, "five generations of the family now rest."

Meanwhile, Reymer drove to the home he shared with his mother, Agnes, at 4638 North 14th Street and blurted out, "Mama, I've just killed a man….I've gone berserk….I'm going to kill myself." After a few minutes, he rushed out of the house with a parting "I love you" and took off again in his car while his frightened mother called her minister. The clergyman advised her to call the police immediately, and they soon responded to the scene. A little after midnight, the police found his car abandoned at North 13th Street and Wakefield, three blocks from his home. Inside was a loaded .25-caliber pistol (not the murder weapon) and several knives.

Police quickly issued a multistate dispatch to be on the lookout for Reymer, in which he was described as white, 5 foot, 8 inches, 165 pounds, with a dark complexion and dark eyes. Virginia State Police joined the Arlington Police in searching nearby woods, aided by a police dog that tracked Reymer two blocks north and one block west to Glebe Road, where it lost the scent at a bus stop.

Around 11:45 p.m., Reymer made a bizarre call to Wayne Oliver (where he placed the call from is unclear), the father of his victim, and "begged for forgiveness." (Given that he claimed to have never met James Oliver, it's also unclear how he knew what name to look up in the phone book.) With remarkable poise, Mr. Oliver told Reymer, "I forgive you. I don't want to see you die. For God's sake give yourself up. Get some treatment." Reymer hung up the phone and then dialed the number to the Bell house and announced that he was "not through killing yet" before abruptly hanging up. Police were alerted to the call, and an officer was posted at the Bell residence to offer protection. Reymer continued his strange odyssey by going to the Carlyn Towers Apartments at 4390 Lorcom Lane and spending the night in the basement elevator shaft after he "apparently attempted suicide" with a piece of broken glass police later found covered in blood. It was a half-hearted attempt that generated a minor cut on the left side of his neck.

The presumably bleeding Reymer awoke several hours later and took a bus to the Ambassador Hotel in Washington, D.C. His mother, Agnes, received two calls from him after he arrived at the hotel, asking her to meet him, adding that he would kill himself if she called the police. Despite this threat, his mother quite reasonably called the police, who went to the hotel, followed by her and another son, only to find that Reymer had departed. In fact, that morning, the twenty-eighth, Reymer turned himself in. In a surreal scene, he took a cab to the Arlington police station located behind the county courthouse. Walking in, he calmly set the murder weapon down on a counter, one round still loaded. Commonwealth's Attorney William J. Hassan happened to be standing next to the counter and, recognizing him from the description issued by police, asked, "Are you Reymer?" When he replied, "Yes," Hassan informed him, "We want to talk to you upstairs." Several women filling out accident reports and applying for permits at the same counter looked on in bewilderment. One startled woman said, "I thought maybe this was the place where they got guns registered" after seeing Reymer lay down his weapon.

Right: James "Bud" Oliver was a talented musician, pictured here with his high school band. He is seated in the middle row, second from the right. *From the 1963 Wakefield High School Yearbook.*

Below: The Bell house still stands watch over the spot where James Reymer forced his way into Oliver's car. *Author's collection.*

Within forty minutes, Reymer was in front of the judge for an initial hearing, and he dramatically fainted, lying on the floor for ten minutes as court officials tried to revive him. As he was hauled off to Arlington Hospital prior to being booked into jail, he was sniffing an "ampule of ammonia" to keep him conscious. At the hospital, his self-inflicted neck wound was stitched up, and he was treated for shock. Dr. John R. McGreevey visited him in the hospital to give an initial mental exam before Reymer's next hearing. When the police came to pick Reymer up, he stubbornly "refused to cooperate" and declined to dress himself. Not to be dissuaded, officers pulled off Reymer's hospital gown and dressed the pathetic man themselves. With Reymer still refusing to cooperate, officers put the "limp and listless" killer into a wheelchair and pushed him out of the hospital.

Arriving at the Arlington County Courthouse, a burly detective with the wonderfully Dickensian name of Jackey R. Snoots hoisted Reymer over his shoulder and carried him into the courtroom. At the hearing, Reymer "acted as if he did not understand the proceedings," with "his

An enraged Reymer forced Oliver to stop at this spot and then killed him. Reymer's childhood home lies directly ahead. *Author's collection.*

eyes fixed into space….An occasional shudder ran through his body."
Commonwealth's Attorney Hassan wanted Reymer committed to
Southwestern State Hospital in Marion for mental tests that normally took
forty-five to sixty days. Reymer's defense attorney, T. Brooke Howard (Skip
Ward's old attorney), wanted more time to talk to his client before testing
began. A committal date was agreed on, and Reymer arrived at the mental
institution on February 4.

Upon arrival at Southwestern State Hospital, Reymer repeated his
previous hospital performance and was "uncommunicative" on his first
day with doctors. His charade didn't last long, and "the next morning he
began to converse freely and showed no unusual symptoms thereafter."
Evaluations were completed by May 26; doctors found him mentally
competent. Reymer claimed to the doctors that "I felt like my mind was
blowing up" for several weeks before the shooting, but they had no trouble
determining that he was sane. Dr. Joseph Blalock summarized his findings
when said Reymer had a "sociopathic personality disturbance" but was

Reymer spent a bizarre night in the basement of Carlyn Towers, at that time a nearly new
building. *Author's collection.*

sane. Reymer returned to Arlington to attend his hearing scheduled for June 23, with no bond set. The police wisely brought along a stretcher in case Reymer decided to repeat his fainting act. Obviously disappointed that an effective insanity defense wasn't feasible, defense attorney Howard "strongly assailed" the hospital testing, saying the doctor there hadn't seen police reports and got most of his information from news reports. Regardless, an arraignment followed in October.

Investigators and the media quickly explored James Theodore Reymer's background, finding an unsavory picture of a man with a considerable criminal record. Born on April Fool's Day 1933, his trouble began in 1947 when he was arrested for car theft in Norfolk, leading to a three-year suspended sentence and probation. He could not stay out of trouble, and a probation violation resulted in a two-year stint at the National Training School, a youth correctional facility. Released in May 1950, he stayed off the police radar only until July 1951, when he was a suspect in a Washington, D.C. robbery. Avoiding a charge, he successfully graduated from Washington-Lee High School, evidently hiding his past from classmates. After graduating in 1952, his troubling behavior reemerged, and he next appeared in an Arlington court in February 1954

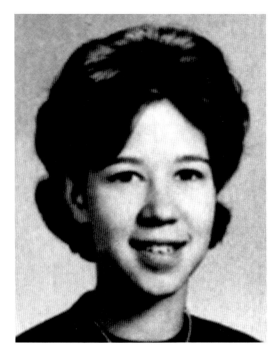

Oliver's date was eighteen-year-old Bonnie Bell, whom he knew from their musical endeavors. *From the 1964 Washington-Lee High School Yearbook.*

James Reymer in happier times, posing with his co-winner of "Most Talented" at Washington-Lee High School, future actress Shirley MacLaine. *From the 1952 Washington-Lee High School Yearbook.*

on an attempted rape charge, but the case was dismissed. His reprieve was short-lived, as in September of that year he was busted for draft evasion, earning him a stint in the Petersburg Federal Reformatory until April 1956. He managed to acquire a wife amid these tribulations but was twice put on one-year peace bonds after domestic arguments, and his fed-up wife divorced him in 1958.

As for his relationship with Bonnie Bell, Reymer "spent most of his life" at 5110 North 6th Street and first met Bonnie, as she lived nearby, apparently, as a newspaper reporter discovered from neighbors, "shortly before her 14th birthday." Although Reymer and his mother eventually moved a short distance away following the death of his father, a relationship with Bonnie developed about two years before the crime. Reymer could clearly be charming and friendly, so perhaps it is not surprising that an impressionable teenager could be enamored of the older man. It's not clear how much of his troubled past that Reymer shared with her, particularly the fact that he had been married before. For her part, Bonnie said that social pressure to have a boyfriend made her date Reymer. Initially, Bonnie's parents were not disturbed when Reymer came over to their house to sing while Bonnie played the piano, and Mrs. Bell said that they thought Reymer was younger than he really was, based on his looks. Although he was "nice and well-mannered," neighbors quickly filled Mr. and Mrs. Bell in on Reymer's criminal and marital past. Not surprisingly, once it became clear that Reymer had romance in mind, they were not happy with the match and refused to let Reymer into their home. When Reymer persisted in the relationship, Bonnie's father, Ivan, got a restraining order for him to stay away from their property. However, she admitted that she kept seeing Reymer "long after" her parents told her not to and that Reymer purchased a marriage license after discussing it several times with her.

Reporters found the Reymers' previous address but evidently not the current one, for they descended on the owner of their old residence, and a steady stream of cars kept driving by for a look. The homeowner said he didn't know Reymer but noted that Bonnie Bell's brother was their paper boy, and he knew Oliver by reputation from Wakefield High School. As he observed, Oliver "graduated from Wakefield before I started there…but he was so popular and so active, everyone's heard of him." Other sources confirmed that Reymer and Oliver did not know each other.

However, there was another side to James Reymer, and in the media, he was variously described as a "hillbilly singer," "country singer" or "folk singer" who played guitar and trumpet. It was also noted that he wrote and collected folk songs. As a senior at Washington-Lee High School in 1952, he was voted "Most Talented," and his yearbook declared that he "stole the gals' hearts with his smile and songs." Referring to him as the school's Eddy Arnold, he was described as having an "easy-going personality" and being a "hill-billy songster." His female co-winner of the "Most Talented" title was Shirley MacLean Beaty, who would soon assume her stage name of Shirley MacLaine and go on to great fame. By the time of the trial, she was well-known enough to be mentioned in several articles about the case. Reymer was considered an "above-average musician" on the guitar and trumpet and was reported to be "well known in Virginia music circles." Despite her well-founded objections to his relationship with her daughter, Bell's mother said Reymer was "really very good" and as good as professional singers. She also thought that he wanted Bonnie to accompany him professionally on the piano.

He moved to Nashville in early 1963 and for the next several months apparently went into several recording sessions under the stage name of Jimmie McLean (presumably inspired by Shirley) but didn't succeed in getting a record contract. Apparently, he played as a musician on several jazz recordings, so perhaps buried deeply in the credits of an obscure jazz record is the name "Jimmie McLean." Admitting defeat in his musical endeavors after his sojourn in Nashville, he took a job as an apprentice television repairman at a shop in Centreville, where his boss described him as "smart but impulsive."

His sojourn in Nashville did not interrupt his relationship with Bonnie, and defense attorney Howard presented fifteen love letters written by Bell while Reymer was at the Nashville YMCA between March and October 1963 during his unsuccessful attempt to start his musical career. Mr. and Mrs. Bell also recalled receiving a series of annoying hang-up calls during the time Reymer was in Nashville and now thought that he was behind the calls. Howard also introduced "a white woolen scarf" that Bonnie made and delivered to Agnes Reymer's house ten days before the murder. The note read: "This scarf I made myself for you to remember me. Bye for now. I'm so glad to see you're studying. Strive hard for Him as I will. Don't call the house. It will cause trouble. I'll be with you in your heart as you are in mine. Love, Bonnie." The references to studying and striving were evidently related to Bell's Jehovah's Witnesses faith, which Reymer had become involved with after he started dating her. Other letters referred generally to marriage plans. Something must have occurred to change Bell's mind in the days after delivering her scarf to Reymer, because she claimed to have broken up with him seven or eight days before the killing. Despite the apparent marriage plans, Bonnie said that Reymer "had a deeper feeling for her than she had for him."

Some insight into Reymer's thoughts after the breakup were gleaned from his boss at the Centreville TV repair shop he worked at, who recalled that the day before the murder Reymer acted "much like an expectant father." The boss had teased him about Bell having another boyfriend, but he said Bonnie wasn't that kind of girl. Based on their conversations, he thought Reymer was secretly married to Bonnie. Reymer told him "little Bonnie's a nut, but I still love her" and, much more ominously, that he would have to "straighten some things out with the girl." In those few days after Bell broke off their relationship, Reymer internalized his jealousy and rage, with deadly results.

Reymer's trial was set for January 4 following his October arraignment hearing. Bonnie was now attending the University of Alabama, and the judge tried to schedule it during her holiday break. Understandably, Bonnie's father described her as "very upset" at having to testify. The trial itself was anticlimactic, as Reymer pleaded guilty to second-degree murder on the condition that it could not be raised to a higher degree. Commonwealth's Attorney William J. Hassan accepted the plea, as he frankly stated that he did not believe he would get a first-degree murder conviction in a jury trial due to Reymer's "psychiatric profile." Proceedings leading to his February 17 sentencing thus focused on determining how long Reymer would be imprisoned. Even though he was declared to be sane, Reymer's mental state was the primary consideration when it came to arguing for his sentence. Howard argued that Reymer operated under a "mad rage of jealousy" and was "acting like a robot" but "under what I consider the antiquated laws we have in this State it is a waste of time to come into court with an insanity plea" unless you had a "raving maniac" to bring into court.

In support of this, his mother testified that he seemed perfectly normal in the days before the crime and was making plans for the future, as seen by his purchase of a new car. It was never made clear how much she knew about his relationship with Bonnie. After the murder, Agnes Reymer insisted that her son's mind was truly blank, and she had to tell him that he had committed the murder. Reymer's brother-in-law, a Baptist minister, claimed that Reymer was detached from reality while in custody, and when he asked him what was wrong, he said, "I've shot myself." He supposedly believed that he was in a car with Bonnie coming back from her school rather than being in custody. When asked on the day of his arraignment if he knew what was going to happen, he said, "Yes, I guess they're going to bury me." The reader can decide how much of this was an act and how much was genuine mental confusion. Also rather dubiously, he testified that Reymer was "looking for religious truths and working in various church groups," although there apparently was a certain amount of truth in this, given Bonnie's efforts to instruct him in the Jehovah's Witnesses faith.

In addition, Howard complained that Southwestern State Hospital doctors spent only three hours interviewing Reymer before declaring him sane (but did not explain how he spent his remaining weeks at the hospital if he wasn't at least being observed). Howard offered his own amateur psychiatric evaluation when he said that Reymer "had to identify with somebody, that he had to lean on somebody," and he identified with Bonnie, on whom "he was completely and entirely dependent." He did have to concede that Reymer knew right from wrong. Commonwealth's Attorney Hassan countered that "the time has long passed when Reymer should have become a man" and, quite inarguably, that "he knows of no legitimate love that brings a man to a woman with a gun in his hand."

Through all of this Reymer sat quietly, "chewing on the back of his knuckles and his fingernails." On February 17, Judge Walter T. McCarthy handed down his decision and sentenced Reymer to the maximum of twenty years; he would receive credit for the year already spent in jail. Judge McCarthy rather curiously said the case could well have been first-degree murder except for "absence of motive and lack of malice toward the victim." There was a very obvious motive (jealousy) and obvious malice (Oliver was the guy on a date with his ex-girlfriend). Reymer, not very convincingly, told the judge that "I would be glad to give my life if it would bring him back," although one doubts the complete sincerity of his statement. With nothing left to do, he embraced his two sisters as he left the court and kissed his mother, saying simply, "Goodbye, Ma." Reymer was evidently paroled in time to marry in 1977, and he had two children. Working as a toolmaker and designer for Tempco Engineering in Reseda, California, he died at the age of fifty-nine in June 1992.

"SORRY, SIS, I HAVE KILLED A GIRL"

n August 1964, murder saw the killer provide a truly unique excuse for his crime. The path to that excuse started when Sherman William Phillips Jr., the twenty-five-year-old son of the pastor of Arlington's Macedonia Baptist Church, spent an evening with sixteen-year-old Norma Alberta Burrill of 511 Shreve Street in Falls Church. Burrill was a junior at Falls Church High School, and her father worked as a file clerk at the Pentagon. For his part, Phillips was described as an "unemployed laborer," and as tended to happen in this era, papers noted that "Phillips is a Negro, as is the victim." He also had apparently spent some amount of time in the army. What the history between the considerably older Phillips and the teen might be was open to interpretation. Later, Phillips's defense attorney claimed rather unconvincingly that it was a "father-daughter" relationship.

Around 1:00 a.m. on August 30, 1964, Phillips and Burrill left a house party on School Lane in the James Lee "Negro community," where they had "quarreled." Witnesses later said he "forced her into his car," but evidently no alarm was raised until police received a call about 10:00 a.m. telling them where they could find a body. Directed to a dirt lane leading to a baseball diamond near Luther Jackson Middle School off Gallows Road (the area is now developed and the baseball field long gone), Lieutenant John Wahl and Sergeant Walter Hook found the body of Norma Burrill "in a clump of bushes." They saw evidence of a struggle, and the "girl's underclothing and stockings had been torn off" and were found nearby.

After finding out who she had last been seen with, a warrant was issued for Phillips and the search for him began.

The search proved to be somewhat unnecessary. Early on the morning of the killing, he went to his sister's house at 508 Shreve Street, just doors away from the Burrill residence being at 511 Shreve Street. "Sobbing" and "hysterical," he penned a note to his sister. It read: "Sorry, Sis, but this is it. I have no one to live for. I have killed a girl. Please, please."

Then he paid a visit to his girlfriend Lillie Mae Herbert of Falls Church at her apartment about 4:00 a.m. In what must have been the sign of a truly desperate man, he asked her for money "so he could go to New Jersey." Herbert later testified that he "said he'd done something awful. He said he had killed a girl. He was very upset and was nervous and crying." Phillips confirmed going there and that he then went back to the ballfield to check on the body because "I couldn't believe she was dead." He must not have been too concerned, as prosecutors would later claim that he also "picked up a girl in Manassas" for a visit. He then drove a little over forty miles west to the town of Marshall, where he went to the cabin of

what was variously reported as a friend or uncle. While there, he called his father, who in turn immediately called the police. They soon arrived at the cabin and arrested Phillips. Initially, he denied the crime until taken to the scene, where he confessed and pointed out the spots where the body had been and her clothes had been disposed of.

A preliminary hearing was held in February 1965, and the case was sent to a grand jury; an indictment followed in March. The trial began in late July, and Phillips entered a guilty plea; it remained for Judge Arthur Sinclair to hear testimony and determine whether the conviction would be for first- or second-degree murder. Phillips

Sixteen-year-old Norma Burrill was the victim of a debauched older man who took advantage of her. *From the 1963 Falls Church High School Yearbook.*

told his version of the story. According to him, he knew Burrill for four or five months before he met her at the house party on the night of August 29. There, she said she wanted to talk to him and willingly got into his car, which contrasted sharply with the witness statements about him forcing her into his vehicle. Then he said they drove to a service station to buy sodas and drove to the baseball field to talk but wound up having intercourse. This issue seems to have been largely sidestepped later on. There never seems to have been any doubt between the autopsy and discarded clothing that a sexual encounter occurred, but evidently there was no direct evidence of rape, so Phillips's story of a consensual encounter was rather dubiously accepted. Why the strong implications of torn undergarments and stockings were ignored will never be clear. The reader will have to decide in light of Phillips's future testimony how believable they find his story of the encounter. Further, how this admission of intercourse fits into his later claim of a "father-daughter" relationship with Burrill was conveniently avoided.

Phillips explained his unique take on how the death occurred. He claimed Norma said she was suicidal after discovering that she was pregnant, and Phillips took pains to point out that it was by her "regular boy friend," not him. Her autopsy showed that she was not pregnant; whether this was a lie on the part of either Phillips or her or she genuinely thought she was pregnant can never be known. Phillips said he "wanted to scare her to get the suicide notion out of her head....She was upset and crying. She said she was going to take her life....I thought at that time that if I could confront her with it—scare her about taking her life—that she would snap out of it." To that end, he said he decided to strangle her so she would see how frightening death would be and then presumably stop just before she passed out. In his remarkable view, he wanted to "teach her the value of life." As he explained it, "I put my hands on her neck and applied pressure. She didn't struggle or say a word. I thought she had fainted." Even more unbelievably, he claimed that she didn't struggle, and when he took away his hands, she placed them back around her throat. A few minutes later, he thought he "heard a sound like someone sleeping...some air escaping. I teased her, but there was no response. That's when I started getting scared." He pulled the body from the car and put it near the dirt lane and drove to his sister's house, where he penned the strange note.

Assistant Commonwealth's Attorney Myron C. Smith called two psychiatrists from Central State Hospital in Petersburg to testify that Phillips was sane. Dr. Leo E. Kirvan said he was a "sociopath, having a personality disorder," but there was "no question that he could distinguish between right and wrong." The defense called Dr. F. Regis Reisenmann (who seems to have been something of a defense witness-for-hire, as he appears rather frequently in cases of the period), who agreed he was a sociopath but stated that it was "recognized as a mental illness." It was also noted during the exchange that Phillips had an IQ of 81. It should be noted that a reporter attending the trial observed that "during his testimony, Phillips appeared calm, but laughed frequently." Reisenmann also addressed Norma's cause of death. Dr. William F. Enos, the Fairfax County medical examiner, testified that the cause of death was "suffocation and/or strangulation," although no marks or bruises were found on her neck and no neck or throat bones broken. In fact, he said that there "was no cause for sudden death of the healthy, young girl." Under cross-examination by defense attorney Thomas Monroe, Enos said the hyoid bone is typically fractured in strangulation but was not in this case. Dr. Reisenmann seized on this and said that in his opinion the death "doesn't appear to me to be strangulation per se," adding that death could have come from cardiac arrest. Suggesting that he knew to deliver exactly what the defense wanted, he added that death could have come from a reflex action "on the part of a person who wanted to die." However, he did concede that in 50 percent of strangulation cases, the hyoid bone is not broken.

Closing arguments wrapped up on July 30. Before sentencing, Phillips conveniently became a bit more remorseful, saying, "I'm sorry to Mr. Burrill and I hope that he can get an understanding with my parents.…It was my mistake." Prosecutor Smith asked for a first-degree murder conviction because it was a "deliberate, willful, premeditated act.…He snuffed out her life and left her lying there in the ballpark." Smith added that he "didn't take her home, he didn't take her to the hospital, or to a doctor." Smith also noted that premeditation could be of short duration—a moment or two before he strangled her. Defense attorney Thomas Monroe claimed exactly the opposite and asked that charges be reduced to involuntary manslaughter due to a lack of malice or premeditation. Monroe claimed, obviously on the word of Phillips, that on a previous occasion he had talked Burrill out of suicide. Monroe stated that "no intent is shown in the evidence, and it cannot be presumed. There was a close, father-daughter relationship between the two and the defendant had never been violent with her before." Again, how the claim of a father-daughter relationship fit with Phillips's statement that he had intercourse with Burrill just prior to the murder was left unexplained by Monroe. The fact that there "was no sign of a struggle" or "no marks on the girl's neck" was used to support Phillips's tale. Monroe also claimed that Phillips's return to the scene of the crime showed remorse and that two witnesses had seen him upset after committing the crime. As further mitigation, Phillips said he drank beer and two pints of vodka during the day before the killing and smoked "about five marijuana reefers." Sinclair asked him if he was drunk at the time of the killing, and he said, "No, man, I wasn't drunk, but I was walking light, you know." The obviously patient Judge Sinclair then asked Phillips if he was satisfied with his defense and if he wanted to call more witnesses. Phillips said he was satisfied but wanted to call one of Burrill's girlfriends; in response, Sinclair said her testimony would have been inadmissible hearsay.

Remarkably, Phillips's strange explanation of the crime seemingly swayed Judge Sinclair to some extent. Phillips was convicted of second-degree murder with a sentence of twenty years. The judge said he "was not satisfied" by the commonwealth's evidence, and there were "too many unknowns" for a first-degree conviction. The reader will have to decide if they agree with Sinclair's conclusion. Norma Burrill is buried at Arlington National Cemetery due to her father's army service in World War II. Following his release from prison, Sherman Phillips lived until 1996 and is buried at Quantico National Cemetery.

"A MIXED UP RELATIONSHIP"

Police responded to a phone call reporting a shooting on March 18, 1966, at 2613 South 9th Street in Arlington. As they began to investigate the scene, a pickup truck pulled up and Thomas Eugene Daniels stepped out. "I'm him," he announced to the surprised police officers. Moments earlier, he had shot to death his sister-in-law, twenty-one-year-old phone operator Elsie Mildred Daniels. Time would prove there was much more to their relationship.

Elsie was married to Thomas's brother David, but they had been separated for seven months; their two children lived with David. Later information showed that there had been previous separations as well. At the time of her death, Elsie rented a bedroom at the home of George and Anna Funkhouser. Mrs. Funkhouser provided much of what was known about the killing. According to her, around 3:45 p.m., a man she had never seen arrived, entered her home and started up her stairs. Shortly afterward, she heard an exclamation of "Oh!" and a noise like a body falling. Although she claimed she didn't hear gunshots, she "sensed that something was wrong and ran next door to a neighbor." After that, the man left her house, at which time she returned and called upstairs to Mrs. Daniels. No reply came in return, and she phoned her husband at work; he took about twenty minutes to arrive. Upstairs, he found Elsie's body on her bedroom floor, shot six times with a .32-caliber Smith & Wesson revolver. An autopsy later showed that Elsie had five bullets in her brain and one that hit her left arm before entering her ribcage and hitting a lung. Mr. Funkhouser called the police, and soon after their arrival, Thomas Daniels made his dramatic appearance. Thomas, a steamfitter, arrived in a company truck, escorted by a police car. After initially fleeing the scene, he had a change of heart and flagged down a patrol car, explained his situation and drove back to the scene with the police following him.

After his sudden appearance and arrest, Thomas Daniels filled in some of the gaps of the story. He said he purchased the murder weapon two weeks prior and had fired it only once before by taking potshots with a friend at the Bailey's Crossroads Hot Shoppe's clock. According to him, he had been drinking since early in the morning of the murder and had called Elsie from a bar. In Thomas's telling, Elsie invited him to come over to her room to "discuss his commitment to her living expenses." He did not explain why he needed a revolver to have that discussion. On his arrival, Thomas said that there was an argument between him and Elsie in the downstairs living room, where Mrs. Funkhouser and one of her children were present. Elsie was ironing, and after some words were exchanged, she "poked the iron at him." Elsie stormed up to her room, calling down, "Don't come up here!" as Thomas pursued her. Ignoring her, he went upstairs, and a short time later Mrs. Funkhouser heard the thudding sound that prompted her flight from the house. Daniels stated that he first shot Elsie in the body, and then in an eerie scene he sat down, cradled her head in his lap and pulled the trigger five more times. Conveniently, he later claimed to have no memory at all of the shooting. Even more implausibly, he claimed that "he did not know the gun was in his pocket" when he arrived.

A motive began to appear, as initial information surfaced about how Elsie was "spurning advances" from Thomas, whose bond was set at $100,000. Supposedly he had "been trying to date her, but she apparently had refused on several occasions." Things became clearer when it emerged that Elsie had in fact been in a relationship with Thomas and had lived with him. He later claimed that his brother had left Elsie three years prior; Thomas then moved in with her, soon fathering a daughter with her. This apparent love child was only briefly mentioned once again in press coverage, and it's unclear who the child lived with. By his own account, Daniels lived with Elsie "off and on" for three years, and apparently they were in an "off" period when the shooting occurred.

Thomas was indicted on June 14, and in October he appeared at a hearing, where he pleaded not guilty, but changed his plea to guilty on October 18 and waived a jury trial. It was then up to Judge Walter T. McCarthy to determine whether he was guilty of first- or second-degree murder. Judge McCarthy opted for a first-degree conviction, and at the December sentencing, Judge McCarthy said the "mixed up relationship with the decedent" was the most important factor in sentencing. The defense had asked for a five-year sentence, and the prosecution asked for a life sentence. Judge McCarthy took the middle ground and sentenced Daniels to thirty years with the statement that the defendant "ought to be caged because he is dangerous," adding that his "rebirth is going to be painful and long." He added Thomas also had past felony convictions and his behavior was "getting worse instead of better." Daniels would be eligible for parole after serving one-quarter of his sentence. Thomas did have one unexpected ally in court; Elsie's husband, David, was at the sentencing and asked for leniency, providing an appropriately bizarre coda to the whole situation when he said that there was "no family problem" that Elsie had lived with Thomas. After all, she was "the only girl he ever really loved."

DEATH AT THE AIRPORT

An airport is far from the most common location for a homicide, but fatal shots rang out in the terminal of National Airport (today's Ronald Reagan National Airport) early on the morning of November 17, 1967. In the nearly deserted North Terminal, a "young, blond-haired" man was seen talking to twenty-eight-year-old Paul Everett Ayres of Woodbridge, employed as a ticket agent by National Airlines. Only a handful of National and Piedmont Airlines personnel were on duty during those early morning hours, and the solitary Piedmont Airlines worker next to Ayres had stepped out to get something to eat, leaving him alone with his visitor at the ticket counter.

Ayres had started his shift at 11:30 p.m., and a couple hours later (as police officials later told the media), one of "several servicemen [who] sat close by in the nearly empty terminal" heard a "sharp report" and saw the man walk away. The ticket agent bent down behind his counter, and the serviceman assumed he had dropped a book and was picking it up. Looking away, neither he nor anyone else noticed that the airline employee did not rise again. Ayres was found lying on his side behind the counter by his boss, station manager William Marterre, as he left for the night between 2:10 and 2:15 a.m. He was still alive but not responsive. Since "[No] one else was there" in the deserted terminal, Marterre had to leave Ayres while he went to get help. Marterre found a sailor in the lobby of the North Terminal, and while Marterre called an ambulance, the Good Samaritan went to Ayres's assistance and delivered mouth-to-mouth resuscitation until the airport ambulance, escorted by police, arrived in a few moments. No obvious wound was visible on Ayres, and Marterre assumed he had a heart attack or seizure. Police soon determined that no money or other items were missing from the ticket counter. But on arrival at the Duke Street Alexandria Hospital at about 2:20 a.m., a small gunshot wound was found in his left midsection. Ayres was pronounced dead a few minutes after arriving.

Police had little to go on, and Marterre described Ayres as "a quiet man—spoke little…I know little of his personal life," even though Ayres had been employed for National Airlines for seven years. However, police did not have long to wait to solve the case, as about 11:00 a.m. on the day of the shooting, twenty-nine-year-old graphic arts specialist David Arthur Nelbach showed up at the office of attorney T. Brooke Howard (Skip Ward's attorney), but Howard was out. Nelbach patiently waited until Howard returned at 3:00 p.m. and informed the attorney that he had killed Paul Ayres at National Airport. In fact, Howard was apparently the second person to learn about the murder. Earlier that morning, Nelbach drove to work as normal with his roommate and co-worker, Ellsworth Lane, and in what proved to be a strange commute, Nelbach told Lane that he was in trouble and then blurted, "El, I shot Paul." Presumably, Lane advised him to seek out a lawyer. At some point, Howard called the authorities and informed them of Nelbach's whereabouts. Given that the FBI did not arrest Nelbach until shortly before 10:30 p.m., Howard and his new client likely spent that evening preparing Nelbach on what he should say while in custody. Nelbach was arrested at a home in Alexandria; given that he had a brother residing there, it would be logical that this is where the arrest was coordinated to occur.

Since the crime occurred on government property, Nelbach was charged with "murder on a government reservation" and proceedings would occur in federal court. Howard requested a mental evaluation for Nelbach, clearly angling for an insanity defense. This was opposed by prosecutors, who stated, "I don't think that jealousy can be equated with mental illness." However, the judge agreed with Howard, and Nelbach was sent to St. Elizabeth's Hospital in Washington for a mental evaluation. In a bit of an understatement, the judge noted that a "shooting under these circumstances is not what I call a sign of stability." While committed at St. Elizabeth's for evaluation, the unlucky Nelbach found himself having to forfeit the collateral he put up for a previous driving offense. Arrested on October 28 for "failure to give proper time and attention to driving," he had put up the collateral pending his court case scheduled for November 27. Due to his stay at St. Elizabeth's, he obviously could not make his court date.

Washington National Airport as David Arthur Nelbach saw it in 1967, before its expansion into Ronald Reagan National Airport. *Library of Congress.*

An indictment followed on December 5, and Nelbach entered a not-guilty plea on January 31. When Nelbach's trial opened in late May 1968 at the Alexandria U.S. District Court, the motive soon became clear. Nelbach, a Lorton resident, was estranged from his wife, Patricia "Patty," having separated five months earlier after twelve years of marriage (which if accurately reported means that Nelbach was a youthful seventeen at his wedding, although certainly not terribly uncommon at that time). Patty was previously employed by National Airlines and ten months before the murder began an adulterous relationship with her now deceased coworker Paul Ayres. Following the Nelbachs separation, Patty took their three children and moved to Dallas, Texas, to live with her family. The two lovers also spent two weeks together in an "apartment hideaway," and Patty later admitted to writing Ayres "almost daily love letters." Amid this drama, Nelbach told Ayres "eight or nine" times over several months to stay away from his wife. According to Nelbach, Ayres showed "indifference" to his entreaties, and on one occasion, he grabbed Ayres by the collar, shoved him against a wall and punched his stomach. Nelbach also told Ayres that "he was dragging her down and making a tramp out of her," but Ayres remained "unconcerned." Patty testified to her side of the sordid affair between her and Ayres in what must have been very uncomfortable testimony. Throughout her testimony, Nelbach held his head in his hands and cried. After testifying, she approached him at the defense table, where they "held hands for a moment and whispered quietly" before Patty went to her seat.

Ayres was also married and had two children; Nelbach called Helen Ayres shortly after the separation and asked her to "try to break up this situation." Ayres testified that "David said several times he would kill Paul," but she didn't believe him because she had made similar statements herself. The two stayed in contact, and Helen said they used each other as "crying towels" during their spouses' affair. Making the whole situation even more complex, she admitted that she became "emotionally involved" with Nelbach but claimed that their relationship never got beyond the "kissing stage." Regardless, the triangle certainly seems to have shifted to a quadrilateral at some point.

Nelbach also tried to enlist the help of Patty's mother, Helen Bradberry of Hamilton, Texas, who later said that he called her and asked her to speak to Patty and talk her out of seeking a divorce. Looking for further advice, the night before the shooting, he asked a female friend at the appropriately named Peyton Place restaurant, "What is wrong with me…for my wife to leave me for another man?" Her rather unhelpful advice was to make his wife jealous by getting a girlfriend to "straighten her out." However, things eventually

Top: A postcard of the Washington National Airport terminal gives an idea of how it looked two decades later when David Arthur Nelbach walked in, bent on revenge. *Author's collection.*

Bottom: Nelbach spent time in St. Elizabeth's Hospital in Washington, D.C., for mental observation. *Library of Congress.*

A closer view of the ticket desks shows how Paul Ayres could have lain unobserved in the nearly empty airport before he was discovered by another worker. *Library of Congress.*

appeared to improve between Nelbach and his wife, and a "reconciliation" between the spouses was planned for Christmas Day. However, things were about to go disastrously wrong.

About 1:00 a.m. on November 17, the day of the shooting, Nelbach opened a letter from Patty calling off the planned reconciliation and asking for a divorce; it also revealed that Ayres had paid Patty a visit in Texas. Papers rather delicately but insinuatingly reported that Patty "entertained him" in Texas. Patty admitted on the stand that she had never been serious about a reconciliation. Nelbach's timing was important, because it would set up a "heat of passion" defense given that the shooting occurred only an hour or so after he supposedly read the letter. In his telling, Nelbach said he then went down to his basement and retrieved a pistol without even really knowing why and that he only remembered driving his truck to the airport, entering into the North Terminal and walking past the empty National Airlines counter. When he walked back a few moments later, Ayres was standing there, and then everything went blank for Nelbach. The shooting itself was a complete blank for him; the next thing he remembered was driving away from the airport and throwing the pistol out of his truck window as he drove over a river. (Driving from National Airport to his Lorton home would not involve crossing a river, so either Nelbach had a wandering drive back home or he deliberately drove over the Potomac or Occoquan River to dispose of the murder weapon.) Nelbach then went home and fell asleep.

Howard must have been pleased to have an all-male jury, who presumably would look rather sympathetically on Nelbach's actions against his wife's lover. Dr. Eugene Stammeyer, a psychologist at St. Elizabeth's, said Nelbach was "intellectually superior but emotionally unstable" and was in the top 2 percent nationally of intelligence but "lacked emotional stamina and the ability to stand on his own two feet." However, Howard was not going to let Nelbach's sanity get in the way of his defense strategy. Howard described Nelbach as a "helpless Casper Milquetoast," referencing a meek comic character. He asked, to "what extent should David Nelbach be penalized for being in love?" Despite it being made clear that Nelbach was not mentally ill, Howard argued that Nelbach suffered a "dethronement of reason" due to the letter he received and could not control his actions. For good measure, Howard made sure to paint Patty in as poor a light as possible, calling her a "treacherous, despicable character if there ever was one." Howard's son Blair assisted him in the defense and added that Patty "dangled David like a marionette, writing letters of reconciliation to him while sending love letters to Paul Ayres."

Regarding Paul Ayres, Blair Howard said that he had a "casual, engaging smile" and a "great capacity for lust," and his father argued that a wife-stealer was guilty of "contributory negligence" in his own death under these circumstances. Taking that line of thinking even further, Howard said that Ayres had in effect "committed suicide" through his actions. All of this was really only a small step removed from the old "unwritten law" defense of years past, where it was accepted that a jilted husband was only defending his honor in taking the life of his wife's lover.

For the prosecution, Assistant U.S. Attorney John Schmidtlein tried to counter Howard by saying that Nelbach "left the gate open" for the affair due to his "drag-racing, drinking, and staying out late." That might be fair enough, but he probably misjudged his jury when he added that Patty shouldn't necessarily be blamed for taking a lover because it "might take two or three men to keep her happy, to give her the love that she needs." Of course, there was no debate that Nelbach shot Ayres; everything came down to his level of responsibility based on his state of mind. Howard argued that an involuntary manslaughter verdict was appropriate while U.S. Attorney C. Vernon Spratley argued for a first-degree murder conviction, stating that

Nelbach showed premeditation by driving from Lorton to the airport and walking around the terminal for ten minutes before the shooting. He also, quite reasonably, called Nelbach's blackout "a convenient loss of memory."

Following closing arguments, the jury deliberated for a little over three hours before they asked for a clarification about the difference between second-degree murder and voluntary manslaughter. Judge Lewis explained that voluntary manslaughter hinged on "heat of passion" while second-degree murder was unpremeditated but committed "with malice." That obviously answered their question, for less than five minutes after that clarification, the jury returned with their verdict: guilty of voluntary manslaughter. At the August 23 sentencing, Judge Oren R. Lewis said he "couldn't condone" Nelbach's actions: "I might even shut one eye or both eyes if you beat the living hell out of him…but I can't condone taking another man's life for any reason." Judge Lewis sentenced Nelbach to the maximum of ten years in prison as Nelbach wept, and he noted that Ayres also "got the maximum penalty." However, Lewis stated, "I don't think he'll be a menace when he gets out." (This evidently proved to be true; Nelbach and Patty not surprisingly divorced, and he remarried much more successfully in 1973, the union lasting for forty-two years.) Moreover, Lewis gave him the leeway to be paroled "at any time" that he was determined to be rehabilitated, not necessarily waiting until he served the normal one-third of his sentence under federal guidelines. In what seems like a heavy-handed hint, Lewis added, "I wouldn't have any objection if they let you out at an early date." Perhaps the "unwritten law" never did quite die out.

BIBLIOGRAPHY

Chapter 1

Washington Evening Star. "Fairfax Posse Kills Slayer of Two Women." January 10, 1954.
———. "Fairfax Slayer Asked God to Forgive Him." January 11, 1954.
Washington Post. "Berserk Gunman's Victims Tell Story." January 10, 1954.
———. "Cab Driver Runs Amok In Fairfax; Baby Injured." January 10, 1954.
———. "Double Rites for Hacker's Victims Set." January 12, 1954.
———. "Two Women's Slayer Asked Forgiveness." January 11, 1954.

Chapter 2

Fairfax (VA) Herald. "Tragedy at Springfield." April 17, 1959.
Guinn, Muriel, and Aldon Hailey. "Autopsy Fails to Reveal Clue to Family Slaying." *Washington Post*, April 14, 1959.
———. "Matthews Feared Alcoholism, Stopped Drinking, Friends Say." *Washington Post*, April 15, 1959.
Hailey, Aldon. "Matthews Autopsy Set, May Explain Tragedy." *Washington Post*, April 13, 1959.
Lawson, John, and Albon Hailey. "Father Kills His 3 Children, Slays Self with Butcher Knife." *Washington Post*, April 12, 1959.

Lee High School. *The Shield.* Springfield, VA: 1958.

McBee, Susanna, and Harry Gabbett. "Tension Led to Tragedy, Pastor Says." *Washington Post*, April 12, 1959.

Miniclier, Kit. "Matthews' Mother Issues Plea for Understanding in Tragedy." *Northern Virginia Sun*, April 13, 1959.

———. "Matthews Widow May Go to Rites." *Northern Virginia Sun*, April 14, 1959.

Northern Virginia Sun. "Funeral Held for Matthews, 3 Children." April 16, 1959.

———. "Is Daughter Tragedy Key, Probers Ask." April 14, 1959.

Rosson, John. "'Shoot Me, Dick!' Slayer Pleaded." *Washington Evening Star*, April 11, 1959.

Washington Evening Star. "Autopsy Fails as Clue to Matthews Tragedy." April 13, 1959.

———. "How the Matthews Family Met Sudden, Violent Death." April 12, 1959.

———. "Letters to the Star: The Mentally Ill." April 15, 1959.

———. "Matthews Case Closed with Motive Unsolved." April 14, 1959.

———. "Mrs. Matthews Goes Home." April 16, 1959.

———. "Tragedy Stills Quartet, Members 'Too Shocked.'" April 12, 1959.

———. "Virginian Kills His 3 Children with Ball Bat, Ends Own Life." April 11, 1959.

Chapter 3

Danville (VA) Bee. "Housewife Admits Fatal Shooting of Her Husband." February 27, 1960.

Kelso, Jack. "Mother of 4 Waits Sentence in Slaying." *Washington Evening Star*, March 1, 1960.

Lillian Chastain, death certificate, January 7, 1965, number 65-001002, Florida Bureau of Vital Statistics.

Miniclier, Kit. "Woman's Plea Is Guilty." *Northern Virginia Sun*, March 1, 1960.

Northern Virginia Sun. "Gun Death Is Declared a Suicide." July 1, 1959.

———. "Husband-Killer Draws 5 Years in Manassas." April 23, 1960.

Washington Evening Star. "Admitted Slayer of Husband Slashes Wrist." March 15, 1960.

———. "Autopsy Report Awaited in Fatal Shooting of Man." June 13, 1959.

———. "Chastain's Death Listed as Suicide." June 20, 1959.

———. "Father Killed; Girl, 2, Found Holding Pistol." June 12, 1959.

———. "Mother Confesses She, Not Child, Fired Gun Killing Her Husband." February 27, 1960.

———. "Mother Gets 5 Years in Husband's Slaying." April 22, 1960.

———. "Virginia Mother Held in Husband's Slaying." February 26, 1960.

Chapter 4

Franklin, Robert. "Jury to Study Weird Shooting." *Northern Virginia Sun*, January 9, 1961.

Northern Virginia Sun. "Drinking Bout Ends in Fatal Shooting of Alexandria Youth." March 2, 1962.

———. "Fairfax Grand Jury Indicts Two on Charges of Murder." September 13, 1961.

———. "Fairfax Jury Indicts 2 on Murder Charges." January 9, 1962.

———. "Frank Jackson Ordered Held For Grand Jury in Killing." August 9, 1961.

———. "Grand Jury Returns 25 Indictments." May 16, 1967.

———. "'Ha, You Missed,' Dying Man Tells Wife Held for Murder." February 17, 1966.

———. "Judge Orders Alexandria Youth Held for Grand Jury on Charge of Murder." April 3, 1964.

———. "Man Convicted and Sentenced in Slaying Case." May 4, 1962.

———. "Man Found Guilty in Pistol Slaying." January 6, 1962.

———. "Man Found Guilty in Slaying." February 21, 1968.

———. "Man Held in Slaying in Dispute Over Beer." November 13, 1961.

———. "Man, 29, Held For Jury in 'William Tell' Death." February 7, 1961.

———. "Murder Trial Off Until Feb. 8." October 27, 1964.

———. "Selecman Given Suspended Sentence." June 20, 1961.

———. "Slaying Suspect Said 'Ideal Boy' by His Father." April 11, 1967.

———. "Youth Faces Grand Jury for Killing." April 29, 1967.

———. "Youth Is Charged in Fatal Beating at Blevinstown." February 6, 1967.

———. "Youth Sentenced in Gun Murder." March 13, 1965.

Washington Evening Star. "Eighty-One Indicted by County Grand Jury." December 1, 1966.

———. "Fairfax Woman Is Held In Death of Ex-Husband." February 17, 1966.

———. "Four Indicted in Fairfax On Murder Charges." March 22, 1966.

———. "Slaying Suspect Is Held for County Grand Jury." December 1, 1966.

———. "Wife Charged with Murder after Husband Dies of Gun Shot Wounds." November 4, 1966.

———. "Youth Held for Fairfax Grand Jury in Slaying." April 29, 1967.

Washington Post. "Youth Indicted In Fatal Beating." May 17, 1967.

———. "Youth Pleads Guilty in Man's Death." February 21, 1968.

Chapter 5

Braaten, David. "Death Probe Turned Quickly to Vinson." *Washington Evening Star*, September 5, 1962.

Douglas, Walter. "Vinson Must Face Adult Court." *Washington Post*, September 8, 1962.

Douglas, Walter, and Everard Munsey. "Young Murder Suspect Has History of Trouble." *Washington Post*, September 5, 1962.

Fairfax (VA) Herald. "Vinson Youth Indicted." September 14, 1962.

Falls Church High School. *The Jaguar.* Falls Church, VA: 1962.

Friedman, Milton. "Rockwell's Poison Leads to Murder." *Jewish News* (Detroit, MI), September 14, 1962.

Griffee, Carol. "Disturbed Youth Home Authorized by Fairfax." *Washington Evening Star*, November 14, 1963.

Hirzel, Donald. "Rabbi Sees Lesson in Goldfein Tragedy." *Washington Evening Star*, September 3, 1962.

Homan, Richard. "Vinson Youth Found Guilty of First Degree Murder." *Washington Post*, May 28, 1963.

Kelly, Brian. "'Peeping Tom' Slayer of Goldfein Gets Life." *Washington Evening Star*, June 22, 1963.

Kelso, Jack, and Jerry O'Leary. "Youth Seized, Admits Killing of Goldfein." *Washington Evening Star*, September 4, 1962.

Martin, Neil. "Vinson Guilty in 1st Degree." *Northern Virginia Sun*, May 28, 1963.

Masley, Peter. "Burned Boy's Father Found Death Weapon." *Washington Evening Star*, September 4, 1962.

McPherson, Myra. "Vinson Fate in Goldfein Slaying to Be Decided June 21." *Washington Evening Star*, May 28, 1963.

Munsey, Everard. "Peeping Tom Shot Youth, Police Say." *Washington Post*, September 2, 1962.

Northern Virginia Sun. "County Delays Action on Pistol Sale Curb." November 8, 1962.

———. "Fairfax Begins Program to Control Sale of Guns." October 5, 1962.

———. "Final Rites Held for Slain Boy." September 3, 1962.

———. "Four Major Cases Go to Grand Jury." September 10, 1962.

———. "Goldfein Slaying Points Up Need of Treatment Center." September 11, 1962.

———. "How Vinson Was Freed Is Probed." September 6, 1962.

———. "Marion Goldfein." June 6, 1963.

———. "Mental Tests Set for Pair." September 11, 1962.

———. "Police Deserve Praise; Revision of Law Needed." September 7, 1962.

———. "Slaying Suspect Held." September 4, 1962.

———. "Study Asks Home for Disturbed." November 2, 1962.

———. "Vinson Enters Guilty Plea." May 27, 1963.

———. "Vinson Papers Found." September 7, 1962.

———. "Vinson's Record Led to Arrest." September 5, 1962.

Platt, Meredith. "When a Teen-Ager Gets in Trouble the Whole Family Needs Help." *Washington Post*, June 27, 1968.

Poole, Daniel. "What Annoys the Boys on a Date." *Washington Evening Star*, March 16, 1962.

Virginia Parole Board. Monthly Parole Decisions. https://vpb.virginia.gov/parole-decisions/.

Washington Evening Star. "Adult Trial to Be Asked for Youth Charged with Falls Church Murder." September 5, 1962.

———. "Mrs. Solomon Goldfein, 45, Mother of Slain Fairfax Boy." June 6, 1963.

———. "Mystery Shots Slay Youth, 17." September 1, 1962.

———. "Peeping Tom Hunted in Fairfax Slaying." September 2, 1962.

———. "Police at Burial of Youth Scan Throng for His Slayer." September 3, 1962.

———. "Police Hunt for Clues in Youth's Death." September 4, 1962.

———. "School Collecting Lewis Goldfein Scholarship Fund." September 8, 1962.

———. "State Seeks 2d Youth In 'Lost' Warrant Case." September 9, 1962.

———. "Trial Set for Youth in Goldfein Slaying." March 13, 1963.

———. "Vinson Indicted As Slayer of Young Goldstein." September 11, 1962.

———. "Vinson Sentenced to Life in Prison for Slaying 18-Year-Old Schoolmate." June 22, 1963.

———. "Vinson Slaying Case Waived by Fairfax Juvenile Court." September 5, 1962.

———. "Youth Faked Name in Buying Murder Pistol." September 6, 1962.

———. "Youth in Goldfein Slaying Pleads Guilty as Trial Opens." May 27, 1963.

———. "Youth Quizzed in Slaying." September 3, 1962.

Wright, Thomas. "Hearing on Gun Law Continued." *Northern Virginia Sun*, March 12, 1964.

———. "Vinson Gets Life Sentence for Murder of Goldfein." *Northern Virginia Sun*, June 22, 1963.

Chapter 6

Barron, John. "Mother to Try to Help Son Held as Slayer of Husband." *Washington Evening Star*, July 10, 1962.

———. "Slaying Plot Warning Came Minutes Late." *Washington Evening Star*, July 5, 1962.

Diggins, Peter. "Bodmer Sentenced to 48 Years for Killing Stepfather." *Washington Post*, May 15, 1963.

———. "Ward Sought to Wed as Jury Argued." *Washington Post*, May 8, 1965.

Douglas, Walter. "Bodmer Found Guilty in Killing of Stepfather." *Washington Post*, February 16, 1963.

———. "Bond Is Denied Bodmer Youth in Slaying of Stepfather." *Washington Post*, July 6, 1962.

———. "Cooley Slaying Plotted 6 Months, Says State." *Washington Post*, July 10, 1962.

———. "Court Rejects Indictment in Cooley Slaying." *Washington Post*, October 10, 1962.

———. "Events at Cooley Slaying Told by Widow on Stand." *Washington Post*, June 19, 1963.

———. "Judge Declares Ward Case a Mistrial." *Washington Post*, March 29, 1963.

———. "Mistrial for Ward Ordered; Jurors Read Newspapers." *Washington Post*, February 17, 1965.

———. "Rehabilitation Home Advised for Bodmer, Stepfather Slayer." *Washington Post*, April 10, 1963.

———. "Stepfather Too Strict, Says Youth in Slaying." *Washington Post*, July 4, 1962.

———. "Ward Convicted in School Teacher Slaying, Sentence Fixed at 40 Years." *Washington Post*, June 22, 1963.

———. "Ward Tells Jury Firing of Rifle Was Accidental." *Washington Post*, March 28, 1963.

———. "Youth Held in Cooley Shooting, Says Gun Went Off Accidentally." *Washington Post*, July 12, 1962.

Griffiths, Harriet. "Teachers, Neighbors Stunned by Tragedy." *Washington Evening Star*, July 4, 1962.

Kelly, Brian. "Ward Jury Dismissed, New Trial to Be Set." *Washington Evening Star*, March 29, 1963.

———. "Ward Murder Case Due to Go to Jury Today." *Washington Evening Star*, June 21, 1963.

———. "Ward Prosecutor Tells Jury It Has 'Obligation to Convict.'" *Washington Evening Star*, March 28, 1963.

Kline, Jerry. "Ward Given Five Years in Teacher Killing." *Washington Evening Star*, May 7, 1965.

———. "Ward Goes on Trial 3rd Time in Slaying." *Washington Evening Star*, February 15, 1965.

Martin, Neil. "Rehabilitation Plan Urged for Bodmer." *Northern Virginia Sun*, April 10, 1963.

McLaughlin, Anne. "Ward Case Goes to Jury Today." *Northern Virginia Sun*, June 21, 1963.

———. "Ward Guilty, Gets 40 Years." *Northern Virginia Sun*, June 22, 1963.

Mount Vernon High School. *Surveyor*. Alexandria, VA: 1963.

Northern Virginia Sun. "Adult Trial Closer For Billy Bodmer." July 17, 1962.

———. "Alexandria Slaying Holds Ward Youth." July 11, 1962.

———. "Bodmer Bail Again Denied." July 10, 1962.

———. "Bodmer Goes on Trial in Stabbing." February 15, 1963.

———. "Bodmer Is Denied Bond in Death of Stepfather." July 5, 1962.

———. "Bodmer Jury Illegal." October 10, 1962.

———. "Bodmer Motion Is Denied." September 26, 1962.

———. "Bodmer Pleads Guilty." February 16, 1963.

———. "Bodmer Pleads Innocent to Murder Charges." October 19, 1962.

———. "Bodmer Trial Delayed for Mental Test." November 15, 1962.

———. "Bodmer Trial Set for Feb. 15." November 15, 1962.

———. "1st Degree Asked in Ward Case." March 26, 1963.

———. "48 Years in Prison for Bodmer." May 15, 1963.

———. "Indictment of Bodmer Is Appealed." September 15, 1962.

———. "Grand Jury Reindicts Boy." October 13, 1962.

———. "Jurisdiction on Bodmer Questioned." September 14, 1962.

———. "Mistrial Declared in Ward Trial." February 17, 1965.

———. "Murder Plan Told by Bodmer." March 27, 1963.

———. "Re-Trial Ordered for Bodmer's Pal." October 13, 1964.

———. "Skip, Billy Not Pals, Wards Say." June 20, 1963.

———. "Skip Ward Gets Five Year Term." May 8, 1965.

———. "State Will Review Ward Case." January 17, 1964.

———. "Ward Calls Shooting of Cooley an Accident." March 28, 1963.

———. "Ward Case Declared a Mistrial." March 29, 1963.

———. "Ward Given 40-Year Prison Term." July 10, 1963.

———. "Ward Goes on Trial in Cooley Death." March 25, 1963.

———. "Ward Goes on Trial 2nd Time." June 18, 1963.

———. "Ward to Be Retried On Same Indictment." October 14, 1964.

———. "Ward to Face Trial June 17." April 9, 1963.

———. "Ward Trial Continued." November 15, 1962.

———. "Witness Testifies Ward Knew of Murder Plans." June 19, 1963.

Redding, William. "Felt Bodmer 'Kidded' on Threat, Ward Says." *Washington Evening Star*, May 6, 1965.

Washington Evening Star. "Billy Bodmer Given 48-Year Sentence." May 14, 1963.

———. "Bodmer Boy Reported Filled with Remorse." July 4, 1962.

———. "Bodmer Faces Trial as Adult." July 17, 1962.

———. "Bodmer Guilty, Awaits Jail-or-Death Decision." February 16, 1963.

———. "Bodmer Says Ward Egged Him On to Attack Bringing Death of Parent." March 27, 1963.

———. "Bodmer Youth Pleads Guilty." February 15, 1963.

———. "Bodmer Youth Pleads Guilty in Stabbing." March 1, 1963.

———. "Bodmer Youth's Trial in Slaying Is Set." January 15, 1963.

———. "Bond Hearing Monday Set in Bodmer Killing." July 6, 1962.

———. "Didn't Believe His Plot, Ward Says of Bodmer." June 20, 1963.

———. "Minister Offers to Place Bodmer In Boys' Home to Avert Jail Time." April 10, 1963.

———. "Mistrial Ruled for Ward; Press Accounts Cited." February 16, 1964.

———. "New Indictment Due in Bodmer Slaying." October 10, 1962.

———. "Six-Month Bodmer Death Plot Charged." July 10, 1962.

———. "Statement at Ward Youth's Trial Describes Role in Cooley Slaying." March 26, 1963.

———. "Teacher Slain, Wife Hurt, 2 Youths Held." July 3, 1962.

———. "Ward Case Review Set In Virginia." January 17, 1964.

———. "Ward Denied New Trial In Teacher Slaying Case." July 10, 1963.

———. "Ward Fired Accidentally, Court Told." July 11, 1962.

———. "Ward Goes On Trial for Second Time." June 17, 1963.

———. "Ward Guilty in Slaying, Gets 40-Year Term." June 22, 1963.

———. "Ward Quoted as Saying Bodmer Planned Killing." June 18, 1963.

————. "Ward's Conviction in Slaying Of Fairfax Teacher Is Upset." October 12, 1964.

————. "Ward Trial Opens; Heavy Penalty Asked." March 25, 1963.

————. "Youth Pleads Not Guilty to Slaying Stepfather." October 18, 1962.

Washington Post. "Billy Bodmer, Accused of Murder, Weeps, Tells Police That He's Sorry." July 5, 1962.

————. "Bodmer Denies Vow to Testify Against Ward." June 20, 1963.

————. "Bodmer Youth Indicted Again." October 13, 1962.

————. "Court Backs Bodmer Slay Indictment." September 26, 1962.

————. "Court Set to Review Ward Case." January 17, 1964.

————. "Death Penalty Asked For Youth in Slaying." March 26, 1963.

————. "Fourth Trial of Skip Ward Is Started." May 4, 1965.

————. "Murder Plan Testimony Given in Ward Case." May 6, 1965.

————. "Murder Trial Ends 2d Day." May 5, 1965.

————. "New Trial Ordered in Teacher's Death." October 13, 1964.

————. "Prison Term for Ward Is Upheld." July 10, 1963.

————. "State Asks Life Term for Ward." May 7, 1965.

————. "Ward On Trial 3d Time in Slaying of Teacher." February 16, 1965.

Chapter 7

Homan, Richard. "Musician Gives Up in Jealousy Slaying of Arlington Student." *Washington Post*, January 29, 1964.

————. "Reymer Transferred from Hospital to Jail." *Washington Post*, January 30, 1964.

Kelly, Brian. "Singer Enters Plea of Guilty in Slaying." *Washington Evening Star*, January 4, 1965.

New York Times. "Reymer, James Theodore." June 10, 1992.

Northern Virginia Sun. "Court Commits James Reymer to Hospital for Mental Tests." January 31, 1964.

————. "Ericson, Eric. Ex-Suitor Sought in Slaying." January 28, 1964.

————. "Girl, 17, Says Former Suitor, 30, Slew Her College Student Friend." July 15, 1964.

————. "Haskell, Robert. Police Carry Confessed Slayer from Hospital." January 30, 1964.

————. "Hillbilly Singer Is Declared Sane, Faces Hearing on Murder Charge." May 26, 1964.

————. "January Set for Reymer Murder Trial." October 16, 1964.

———. "Man Admits Slaying in Love Triangle." January 29, 1964.

———. "Preliminary Hearing for Reymer Continued Again in County Court." June 4, 1964.

———. "Reymer Given 20-Year Sentence for Murder of College Freshman." February 18, 1965.

———. "Reymer Hearing to Be Scheduled." October 13, 1964.

———. "Rites Held Today for James Oliver." January 30, 1964.

Russell, Lee. "Guilty Plea Is Entered By Reymer." *Northern Virginia Sun*, January 5, 1965.

Tuck, Lon. "Murder Suspect Sent to Mental Hospital." *Washington Post*, January 31, 1964.

Wakefield High School. *Startstone*. Arlington, VA: 1963.

Washington Evening Star. "Dated Reymer, Girl Says." July 15, 1964.

———. "Folk Singer Gives Up in Killing." January 28, 1964.

———. "Grigg, William. Reymer Stunned by Events." January 30, 1964.

———. "Jealousy Blamed in Killing." January 28, 1964.

———. "Mother Is Relieved by Son's Surrender." January 29, 1964.

———. "Reymer Able to Face Trial." May 26, 1964.

———. "Reymer Gets 20 Years in Killing of Editor's Son." January 17, 1965.

———. "Singer Ordered to Hospital for Sanity Tests in Slaying." January 30, 1964.

———. "Test of Sanity Is Sought in Student Killing." January 29, 1964.

Washington-Lee High School. *Blue and Gray*. Arlington, VA: 1952.

———. *Blue and Gray*. Arlington, VA: 1963.

Washington Post. "Ayres, B.D. Reymer Pleads Guilty to 2d Degree Murder." January 5, 1965.

———. "Hearing Put Off in Reymer Case Until June 23." June 4, 1964.

———. "Hillbilly Singer Held In Slaying of Student." July 15, 1964.

———. "Musician, 30, Indicted in Boy's Death." October 13, 1964.

———. "Reymer Gets 20 Years for Arlington Slaying." February 18, 1964.

Chapter 8

Buehrer, Judi. "Minister's Son Pleads Guilty in Girl's Death." *Northern Virginia Sun*, July 21, 1965.

Fairfax (VA) Herald. "Recent Deaths." September 11, 1964.

Falls Church High School. *The Jaguar*. Falls Church, VA: 1963.

Griffee, Carol. "Pastor's Son Charged in Fairfax Girl's Death." *Washington Evening Star*, August 31, 1964.

Northern Virginia Sun. "Fairfax Man Held in Slaying." August 31, 1964.

———. "Guilty Plea Entered." July 24, 1965.

———. "Minister's Son Indicted by Jury." March 16, 1965.

———. "Murder Charge Holds Phillips." February 3, 1965.

———. "Murder Trial Is Continued." June 29, 1965.

———. "Phillips Gets Maximum of 20 Years in Girl's Death." July 31, 1965.

Washington Evening Star. "Minister's Son Calls Girl Killing Accidental." July 21, 1965.

Washington Post. "Minister's Son Charged in Strangling of Girl, 16." August 31, 1964.

Chapter 9

Cheek, Leslie. "Estranged Wife Is Slain, In-Law Held." *Washington Post*, March 19, 1966.

Coffin, Sidney. "Daniels Sentenced to 30 Years for Slaying of Sister-in-Law." *Northern Virginia Sun*, December 10, 1966.

Huser, Paul. "Police Hold Brother-in-Law in Phone Operator's Slaying." *Northern Virginia Sun*, March 19, 1966.

Northern Virginia Sun. "Arlington Grand Jury Indicts 53." June 16, 1966.

———. "County Man Convicted in Slaying of Woman." October 21, 1966.

———. "Plea Change Is Made in Slaying Case." October 19, 1966.

———. "Slaying Hearing Scheduled Today." March 23, 1966.

Washington Evening Star. "Arlington Man Found Guilty of Murder." October 21, 1966.

———. "Daniels Files Guilty Plea in Slaying." October 19, 1966.

———. "Man Gets 30-Year Term in Sister-in-Law Killing." December 10, 1966.

———. "Woman Shot Six Times, Man Held for Grand Jury." April 27, 1966.

———. "Woman, 21, Shot Dead, In-Law Held." March 19, 1966.

Washington Post. "Arlingtonian Found Guilty of Murder." October 21, 1966.

———. "Falls Church Man Jailed For 30 Years." *Washington Post*, December 10, 1966.

Chapter 10

Aschenbach, Joy. "Manslaughter Ruled in Slaying by Nelbach." *Washington Evening Star*, May 24, 1968.

———. "Nelbach Gets 10 Years in Slaying at National." *Washington Evening Star*, August 23, 1968.

Kline, Jerry. "Man Indicted in Slaying of Airline Ticket Clerk." December 6, 1967.

———. "Slaying of Airline Agent Called 'Triangle' Case." *Washington Evening Star*, November 22, 1967.

McLaughlin, Maurine. "Doctor, Friends Testify for Suspect in Slaying." *Washington Post*, May 22, 1968.

———. "He 'Cannot Recall' Slaying, Nelbach Sobs in Testifying." *Washington Post*, May 23, 1968.

———. "Nelbach Convicted of Manslaughter in Airport Slaying." *Washington Post*, May 24, 1968.

———. "Triangle Blamed in Slaying." *Washington Post*, November 22, 1967.

Northern Virginia Sun. "Airport Slaying Suspect Will Get Mental Tests." November 23, 1967.

———. "FBI Arrests Suspect in Airport Slaying." November 18, 1967.

———. "Nelbach Indicted." December 7, 1967.

———. "Nelbach Is Given Ten Years." August 24, 1968.

———. "Slaying Suspect Forced to Forfeit Traffic Collateral." November 28, 1967.

———. "Ticket Clerk Death Trial in 2nd Day." May 21, 1968.

Washington Evening Star. "Can't Recall Shooting, Nelbach Says at Trial." May 23, 1968.

———. "Defense Calls Slaying at Airport 'Provoked.'" May 21, 1968.

———. "Doctors Call Nelbach Emotionally Unstable." May 22, 1968.

———. "Man Charged with Slaying at Airport." November 18, 1967.

Washington Post. "Airport Slaying Case Opens." May 21, 1968.

———. "Airport Slaying Suspect Swears He's Innocent." February 1, 1968.

———. "Lorton Man Arraigned in Va. Slaying." November 19, 1967.

———. "Man Given 10 Years in Slaying at Airport." August 24, 1968.

———. "Man Is Indicted in Airport Death." December 7, 1967.

ABOUT THE AUTHOR

Zachary Ford is a high school English teacher in Fairfax, Virginia, and an officer in the Army Reserve. He grew up in a wide variety of places across the country, including Fairfax County. He holds a bachelor's degree in history from the University of Texas at Austin and a master's of education from Temple University. In his spare time, he enjoys visiting the historical sites of the world.